THE HOLY SPIRIT

Other books in the Foundations of Christian Faith series

Believing in Jesus Christ by Leanne Van Dyk

The Christian Life by Michael L. Lindvall

Christian Worship by Ronald P. Byars

Creation and Last Things by Gregory S. Cootsona

Searching for Truth by Thomas W. Currie III

The Trinity by Philip W. Butin

What It Means to Be Human by Michelle J. Bartel

THE HOLY SPIRIT

Mateen Elass

Foundations of Christian Faith
Published by Geneva Press in Conjunction with
the Office of Theology and Worship, Presbyterian Church (U.S.A.)

Book design by Sharon Adams
Cover design by Night & Day Design

First edition
Published by Geneva Press
Louisville, Kentucky

This book is printed on acid-free paper that meets the American National Standards Institute Z39.48 standard. ∞

PRINTED IN THE UNITED STATES OF AMERICA

05 06 07 08 09 10 11 12 13 14 — 10 9 8 7 6 5 4 3 2 1

Library of Congress Cataloging-in-Publication Data

Elass, Mateen, 1955–
    The Holy Spirit / Mateen Elass.— 1st ed.
        p. cm. — (Foundations of Christian faith)
    ISBN 0-664-50137-0 (alk. paper)
    1. Holy Spirit. I. Title. II. Series

    BT121.3.E43 2004
    231'.3—dc22
                                        2004052272

Contents

Series Foreword   vi

A Word about Language   vii

1. Spirituality and the Spirit of God   1

2. Playing Twenty Questions   8

3. Getting Tuned In   15

4. People of the Spirit   23

5. Spirit-Filled Worship?   38

6. The Gift That Keeps on Giving   49

7. Fruitful Lives   63

8. Furrows in the Heart   75

Notes   92

Series Foreword

*T*he books in the Foundations of Christian Faith series explore central elements of Christian belief. These books are intended for persons on the edge of faith as well as for those with strong Christian commitment. The writers are women and men of vital faith and keen intellect who know what it means to be an everyday Christian.

Each of the twelve books in the series focuses on a theme central to the Christian faith. The authors hope to encourage you as you grapple with the big, important issues that accompany our faith in God. Thus, Foundations of Christian Faith includes volumes on the Trinity, what it means to be human, worship and sacraments, Jesus Christ, the Bible, the Holy Spirit, the church, life as a Christian, political and social engagement, religious pluralism, creation and new creation, and dealing with suffering.

You may read one or two of the books that deal with issues you find particularly interesting, or you may wish to read them all in order to gain a deeper understanding of your faith. You may read the books by yourself or together with others. In any event, I trust that you will find a fuller awareness of the living God who is made known in Jesus Christ through the present power of the Holy Spirit. Christian faith is not about the mastery of ideas. It is about encountering the living God. It is my confident hope that this series of books will lead you more deeply into that encounter.

Charles Wiley
Office of Theology and Worship
Presbyterian Church (U.S.A.)

A Word about Language

In the last few decades we have become increasingly aware that traditional theological language, which is often patriarchal and male-oriented, can alienate many who feel marginalized by one-sided gender language and assumptions. Growing sensitivity has brought about new Bible translations that are more accurate by reflecting the original inclusiveness of the biblical texts. So, for example, the generic Greek word *anthrōpos*, which formerly was regularly translated "man/mankind," is now more correctly translated "humanity/humankind."

However, there is still some crucial language in the Bible having to do with God that is masculine in nature. Some wish to do away with this gender exclusiveness, arguing rightly that since God is not part of the created order, and sexuality is, then to use exclusively masculine language for God is to tread dangerously close to idolatry. Solutions offered to this problem include on the one hand the use of both masculine and feminine imagery and language for God, and on the other the avoidance of any gender-specific language at all, speaking of "Godself" rather than utilizing masculine or feminine pronouns.

I am opting in this book to stick with the traditional language for God for the following reasons:

1. The Bible consistently refers to God in personal, masculine terms. If the Scriptures are a true revelation of the nature of God, then the fact that God chose the times, places and cultures within which to reveal that nature ought to indicate that

masculine imagery and address, while not perfect, is the best option we have to envision God correctly within our limited understandings. It would demand a pretty awesome revelation to unseat two thousand years of biblical witness and another two thousand of Christian tradition.

2. "Masculinity" does not equal "maleness." While the latter emphasizes sexual gender and so is tied to created bodies, the former deals with the essential quality behind maleness—that of initiative. Likewise, femininity deals principally with the quality of response or receptivity. These qualities are reflected biologically in form and function of the human sexual organs. Typically, masculinity and maleness go together, but not always. Likewise with femininity and femaleness. When we talk about God, the creaturely categories of male and female go out the window, of course. But not the quality of initiative. God reveals himself overwhelmingly as the one who comes to his creation, or his chosen people, or his chosen servant, and begins a relationship that could be started no other way. This is in part what we mean by calling God sovereign. By contrast, the creation and everything in it is typically seen as feminine when relating to God. It is no accident that Israel is referred to in the Old Testament as the bride of Yahweh, and the church in the New Testament as the bride of Christ, or that the creation is accorded feminine gender. The whole created order was constructed to respond to the loving initiative of God.

3. Based on the Gospels, every time Jesus addressed God in extemporaneous prayer, he used the term "Father."[1] Further, he commanded his followers to make this their typical address for God: "Pray then this way, 'Our father in heaven . . .' " While it is true that from time to time the Scriptures use feminine metaphors or similes to describe God's activity, nowhere is God addressed in the feminine or spoken of in the feminine gender. To refer to God in the feminine as well as masculine today has the potential of introducing confusion concerning the nature of God where there was none in the original revelation given to us.

4. The avoidance of any gender-specific language for God neatly sidesteps most of the above concerns, but it raises fresh problems. Extended conversation about God becomes awkward as

speakers engage in syntactical gymnastics to avoid pronominal references to God. More consequentially, the avoidance of masculine or feminine pronouns in the normal course of conversation has the unintended effect of depersonalizing God for the listener. This inadvertent message of an impersonal God is arguably even more confusing or misleading than that of mixing gender language.

5. It has been suggested that a workable compromise may be found by referring to the first and second persons of the Trinity in masculine terms (since they are traditionally known as Father and Son), and speaking of the Spirit in feminine terms. In support of this it is noted that the Hebrew *ruach* is feminine in gender and some of the biblical images used of the Spirit have feminine overtones (e.g., the Spirit like a mother bird hovering protectively over a fledgling creation; see Gen. 1:2). But of course the gender of a word in Hebrew (as also in Greek) has no necessary connection to the gender of the thing itself. The most likely explanation for *ruach*'s feminine gender is that Hebrew categorizes most of the elements of nature in the feminine gender (sun, earth, rain, etc.). Since one of the principal meanings of *ruach* is wind, the word most naturally follows this pattern. It must also be noted that the Greek word used in the New Testament for "spirit" (*pneuma*) is neuter in gender, and further, that often the biblical writers, against language conventions, use masculine referential pronouns when pointing to the Spirit rather than feminine or neuter pronouns, as grammatical rules would mandate.

Trinitarian thought recognizes that the members of the Godhead share equally in the same divine nature. To speak of two in the masculine and one in the feminine introduces a subtle difference that undermines the essential unity of all three. Likewise, to speak of the Spirit using the impersonal pronoun "it" is unsatisfactory. Not only does this suggest that the Spirit is somehow different in nature from the Father and Son, it also suggests the Spirit is less personal than the other members of the Godhead. The Scriptures as well as the internal logic of the Trinity repudiate this notion.

Therefore, I use traditional Trinitarian language when speaking of God, and masculine pronouns with reference to the Father, Son and Holy Spirit. My hope is that the reader will guard against the error of thinking about God as a man, but nevertheless recognize the deeper meaning inherent in the claim that God's nature is best understood by finite creatures in terms of exemplary masculinity. This is true no less of the Holy Spirit than of the Father or the Son.

1

Spirituality and the Spirit of God

I wouldn't call myself religious, but I'm very spiritual. . . ."
This seems to be the mantra of our times as Americans seek
nontraditional, noninstitutional ways to "connect with God."
It is not that people are necessarily against organized reli-
gion, but the church is no longer seen as keeper of the door
to God's throne room. As all roads lead to Rome, so all
attempts to reach God ultimately succeed. If you are sincere
in your spiritual pursuits, you will find your way to your ultimate goal.

But what does it mean to be spiritual? In past centuries,
spirituality had to do with living in the presence of the Spirit
of God, as understood according to Christian theology and
tradition. But now the term has become so diffuse as to mean
almost whatever its speaker wishes. How-to books on New
Age spirituality have surged to the most prominent shelves in
mainstream bookstores. From learning the secrets of the hidden spirit world to channeling the power of pyramids to inner
healing through crystals, writings abound to accommodate
the most exorbitant interests. Even in contemporary Christian
settings, spirituality has loosed its moorings from traditional
approaches and become a cultural child of the times.

While in traditional Christian spirituality the transforming
power of the Spirit was made available by the work of Jesus
Christ and applied to one's life by the steady practice of disciplines such as prayer, fasting, solitude and worship, much
of modern American spirituality is rather impersonal and

technique-oriented—a curious mix of pseudoscience and technology, mechanistic routines and Eastern philosophical monism. We are told that pyramids distill the quantum energy of the universe, that certain crystals enable our souls to resonate with cosmic harmonic frequencies, that heavenly bliss comes as we discover our oneness with all that is, that the droning repetition of certain syllables opens the center of our being to the universal mind (or, as one bumper sticker has it, "Chant Hare Krishna and be happy"). People who are no longer sure of the existence of a personal God are turning to strategies designed to tap the creative but impersonal energies of the universe. The "Spirit" turns out to be something like the "Force," and spirituality becomes whatever enables me to access it for my own life-enhancing ends.

In the late nineties, a fashion accessory fad took advantage of this trend by marketing "power beads." Found in most major department stores, these bracelets of semiprecious stones were touted as providing what people really need for life. One manufacturer listed the powers and benefits as follows:

> rock crystal—to enhance strength and protect from evil
> rose quartz—to attract love and heal matters of the heart
> tiger's eye—to inspire courage, confidence and strong
>   willpower
> mother of pearl—to attract wealth and money
> amethyst—an energizer for the mind, increasing brain
>   power
> jade—to vivify and increase longevity
> black onyx—to aid self-control, make resolutions a reality
> carnelian—aids passion, enhances human sexuality
> goldstone—to infuse a "super positive attitude"
> hematite—to banish depression and relieve aches
> aventurine—success to achieve goals and make life-
>   enhancing decisions
> turquoise—for good health and well-being.

While officially saying such stones only *represent* the associated qualities, companies such as the one from which this list came marketed power beads so as to imply that wearing certain kinds of rocks on your wrist will mystically produce virtues and blessings that previous generations knew came only through discipline, sacrifice and union with God. Sadly, due in large part to the spiritual confusion of our age and the commonplace human desire to secure benefits with the least amount of effort, power beads sold like hotcakes. They are still available. P. T. Barnum would have loved this hustle.

Contemporary spirituality also often disengages spiritual experience from consequent moral behavior. This is not surprising, given our culture's long-standing love affair with hedonism. Spirituality thus also serves our pursuit of easy pleasure—"Give me bliss, but don't cramp my lifestyle." What one feels or experiences as "spiritual" has no necessary ethical implications, especially ones that would interfere with personal desires.

Such a view stands in stark contrast with biblical spirituality, which asserts in the words of Paul, "If we live by the Spirit, let us also walk by the Spirit" (Gal. 5:25). From a Christian point of view, the goal of spirituality is to create a new heart within us, one that leads us to think and act consistently like Jesus Christ.

Further, modern American spirituality is notoriously privatized and individualistic. In part, this perspective is a cultural remnant of Enlightenment thought, which argued that the realm of religious beliefs falls under the category of values rather than facts and as such cannot be usefully debated in the public square. Metaphysical views were best kept to oneself, or voiced as opinions rather than truths. Today spirituality typically remains in the realm of the private—those interested in life beyond the mundane world are encouraged to follow their inner voice. But what works for one may promise no success for another. As spirituality is increasingly self-defined, so is the path to enlightenment. If there are as many paths as people, then community will not be a necessary element of spiritual life. It is not thereby eradicated from all life, but it is marginalized.

For those who follow Jesus, the life of the Spirit presents a more compelling model. God is indeed concerned with the individual and his or her salvation, so much so that the physical body of a believer is understood as a temple that the Holy Spirit inhabits (2 Cor. 6:19).

However, God is equally concerned with the establishment of a redeemed community of people, one in which love and righteousness are displayed through unity and harmony. It is the community or family of God into which each believer is incorporated when baptized in the name of the Trinity. So this fellowship, the church, is also spoken of as a temple, a building of living stones, inhabited corporately by the Holy Spirit (1 Cor. 3:9–17; Eph. 2:21–22; 1 Pet. 2:5). To grow spiritually is to become more interconnected through the Spirit of Christ with the larger community of those who have given their allegiance to Jesus of Nazareth.

Lastly, modern American spirituality bears the imprint of postmodern thought. Not only is truth privatized ("I believe in the God of the Bible, but that might not work for you"), but it is also stripped of internal logic and consistency. In many cases the quest for real truth ceases to be relevant as seekers stand before a smorgasbord of competing truth claims and embrace mutually exclusive beliefs. It is not unusual to find people who say, "I believe that all is one [monism]," but who also pray to a personal God (separate from them) and/or practice transcendental meditation as a way to evolve independently into a higher life form. In the past, such an illogical eclecticism would have caused seekers to doubt that they had yet gained real wisdom, for internal consistency of beliefs and their correspondence to external reality were important criteria for valid metaphysical viewpoints. In a postmodern world, such is no longer the case.

Over against this, traditional Christian spirituality sits within the context of a comprehensive biblical worldview. The Spirit of God and the revelation of truth are intimately connected. We are shown rather clearly how human beings are called to relate to the created world and its Creator. Since the nature of God and of the created world determine what constitutes authentic spirituality, we cannot simply decide for ourselves "how to be spiritual," especially based on our own feelings or desires. Rather, we must learn who this God is who stands at the center of life, and respond accordingly. For Jews and Christians over the last four millennia, this response has had traceable boundaries and well-founded practices. We will discuss these in subsequent chapters.

But confusion over spirituality is not limited to our non-Christian culture. The church in America also finds itself struggling for understanding in this arena. From "Spirit-filled," unpredictable, charismatic congregations to unorthodox but enthusiastic snake-handling groups to predictably subdued, mainline denominational churches, the people of God are not of one mind as to how to express "Christian spirituality." In large measure this is due to a dearth of knowledge about the Holy Spirit. Particularly for those in Reformed, mainline churches, the Holy Spirit is indeed the forgotten member of the Trinity. Though referred to in our creeds and liturgical prayers, the Spirit does not get much air time in sermons and teaching venues. Many traditional Christians remain ignorant and even apathetic about the Holy Spirit. Because of perceived excesses in Pentecostal, charismatic, and cultic circles, middle-of-the-road Christians often link and limit the Spirit of God to ecstatic experiences such as speaking or singing in tongues, holy laughter, being slain in the Spirit, loud and raucous healing sessions—most of which seem distasteful at best, spurious at worst.

Having lost our biblical moorings, the American church drifts in much the same eddies as the culture around it. Recently, at a Christian burial service, the officiating minister read the following words, purporting to be from the deceased:

> Do not stand at my grave and weep;
> I am not there, I do not sleep—
> I am a thousand winds that blow;
> I am the diamond glints of snow—
> I am the sunlight on ripened grain;
> I am the gentle autumn's rain.
> When you awaken in the morning's hush,
> I am the swift uplifting rush
> of quiet birds in circled flight.
> I am the soft star that shines at night.
> Do not stand at my grave and cry—
> I am not there, I did not die.

Here a thin, comfortless gruel of Eastern monism has been substituted for the strong meat of the gospel. Death is not the enemy defeated by the resurrected Christ; rather it is the frigid friend that takes up the dust of the soul and scatters it to the four winds, where the deceased now animates the physical world, along with, presumably, all the billions already dead. There is no hope of remaining oneself through eternity, of being reunited with loved ones in heaven, of seeing God face-to-face and enjoying unimpeded divine love. All that exists is an impersonal "world soul or spirit" to which our life force is merged; personal identity is annihilated when we die.

Cold comfort this! How tragic that such viewpoints find a home in the church that claims to follow the resurrected Savior. If we are confused about doctrines so central to the gospel message, it cannot be surprising that we are hopelessly lost when it comes to defining spirituality and the Spirit of God. But it is not just doctrinal amnesia that plagues God's people today. We are also beset with moral ambivalence. Taught rightly that we are saved by grace, many of us have concluded that lifestyle actions are not all that important—since God accepts me as I am, his presence presumably will always be with me, no matter how I act.

A few years ago an engaged couple in their midfifties came to me inquiring about being married in the church. Each had been married and divorced twice before, but, as they explained, these marriages had been joined and sundered prior to their "finding God." They were convinced that their present relationship would not end in divorce because, as the man stated, "There are three of us in this relationship: God, my fiancée and me." As we talked further, it came out that they had been living and sleeping together for over six months. I asked them how they could reconcile their behavior with the biblical teaching of chastity before marriage. "Well, it feels so right," they responded. "We feel so close and know that God is with us, so it can't be wrong."

This scene is repeated many times over in congregations today. My aim in sharing this is not to point fingers, but to underscore the fact that even among God's people the link between *holy* and *Spirit* has been severed in day-to-day life. To experience God is one thing; to live according to the will of God is quite another. The two have no necessary connection for many who call themselves Christian.

How, then, does one speak of the Holy Spirit in such a context? Where our post-Christian culture knows nothing of the Spirit's existence, and Christians ignore the Spirit's will in favor of pursuing their own agendas, clear teaching on the person and work of the third member of the Trinity is critical. I hope that this book will convincingly show that true spirituality in the human arena is the province of the Holy Spirit, and that we grow best in our spiritual lives by exposing ourselves to the one whose presence and power draw us toward the perfection for which we were created.

To that end, in the coming chapters we will discuss the identity and work of the Spirit, seeking to answer questions about the Spirit's divinity, relationship to the living and written Word, work in creation and re-creation, ministry in the church and in the individual disciple, and presence in the world around us. As these deeper truths about the Holy Spirit become clear in the minds of God's people, the road to true spirituality will open before us, and we will walk in the newness of life that Jesus Christ died to procure for humanity, and that the Spirit was given to establish.

2

Playing Twenty Questions

*R*emember that game we often played as kids: Twenty Questions? The object was to think of a thing that your friend then had to deduce by asking a maximum of twenty questions. Naturally, the goal was to stump your partner by latching onto something people rarely if ever think about. As I remember, the first question asked was typically meant to quickly limit the field—Is it animal, mineral or vegetable? From there the questions would become more and more focused.

In this chapter our task is to seek to clarify the nature of the Holy Spirit. Perhaps a good start would entail answering the question, Who or what is the Holy Spirit—a force, a thing, a living being, an attribute of God, part of God's good creation, part of God, or God himself by another name? All of these answers have been put forward by religious folk of one stripe or another. Our goal is to uncover what the Bible and orthodox Christian tradition have clearly affirmed.

If one looks principally at the Old Testament, we find mostly a pencil sketch of the Holy Spirit. There are not many times where the Spirit plays a front-and-center role, and in the few instances where such is the case, one could argue that the Spirit of God is simply the power of God extended by the divine hand into the world of human affairs. In the burning bush confronting Moses, and in the pillar of fire protecting and leading the Israelites in the wilderness, we see the dynamism characteristic of the Spirit of God. It is indeed true that the main Hebrew word for the Spirit (*ruach*) can also

8 /

mean "spirit" as the undefined essence of a thing, "breath" as that which enlivens a body, or "wind" as the dynamic movement of air that has varied effects on the environment. Much of the work of the Holy Spirit in the Old Testament belongs to the category of dynamic power and mysterious, sometimes stormy, intervention in the affairs of Israel or the larger world. Wherever the *ruach* of the Lord is mentioned, something active happens—the divine invades our world as sovereign power with moral purpose. Here the Spirit is rarely distinguished clearly from God. Hence some people have concluded that the Spirit is subpersonal, merely a way of talking about God's dynamic work of forming, judging and rescuing his creation or chosen people.

But even in the Old Testament there are hints that the Spirit of God is a conscious, personal being. In the act of creation, the Spirit seems to play a distinctive role, hovering like a mother bird over a formless chaos at the beginning of all things, breathing life into human beings, reviving the dry bones of a spiritually lifeless people (see Gen. 1:2–5; 2:7; Job 33:4; Pss. 33:6; 104:30). God's will for his people is communicated most often through the work of the Spirit, who inspires prophets and empowers leaders. In 2 Samuel 23:2 David asserts that the Spirit of God communicates personally: "The Spirit of the LORD speaks through me, his word is upon my tongue." Those chosen by God for special tasks are filled with the creative Spirit, who graces them with the necessary abilities to complete their service well. This is true of artisans and musicians as well as kings and warriors. The Spirit is also characterized as holy, capable of being grieved by the spiritual rebellion of Israel (Isa. 63:10–11), and of withdrawing from the lives of those toying with sin (Ps. 51:11).

The New Testament, where reference to the Holy Spirit is much more frequent, confirms the personal nature of this Spirit. The Spirit breathes inspiration into human words, and quickens God's people to mission and service. In times of dispute with the authorities, the Spirit gives believers the appropriate words for the moment. In times of confusion within the Christian community, the Spirit speaks with sure guidance (Acts 8:29, 10:19, 11:12, 13:2). The New Testament book of Acts has often been nicknamed

"The Acts of the Holy Spirit" because of the Spirit's work in orchestrating the ministry and mission of the apostles and early converts. Likewise, the Spirit creates community among people where before there had been hate or discord, and stimulates Jesus' followers to a new life. These all constitute the actions of a personal being.

If the Spirit is a personal being, how does this still mysterious figure relate to God the Father and Jesus the Son? Both Old and New Testaments ascribe to the Spirit the kinds of qualities typically ascribed to God: omnipresence, goodness, unchanging nature, sovereign power, eternality, omniscience and holiness. The Spirit is frequently referred to as the Spirit of God (or the Lord) and sometimes as the Spirit of Jesus. Even more compellingly, Jesus accords the Spirit the same status as he sees for himself. When teaching the disciples about his impending departure and seeking to ease their confusion and grief, he assures them that he will not leave them orphaned, as it were, but will ask the Father to send them "another advocate" to continue his ministry in their lives (John 14:16–18). That the Spirit is a second advocate presumes Jesus as the first advocate. This account suggests that the Spirit would continue what Jesus has begun in his followers, because the Spirit owns the same divine nature and mission as Jesus. This conclusion is supported by the Greek word translated into English as "another." Ancient Greek provided two possible words to convey the idea of "another": *heteros*, meaning "another of a different kind" (from which we get English words such as "heterosexual" and "heterodox"); and *allos*, meaning "another of the same kind" (from which we get words such as "allogenic" and "allopathic"). In speaking of the Spirit, Jesus used this latter word, and so emphasized to the disciples that as they had been secure in his hands, they would remain so in the Spirit's care. Whatever blessing they had known in Jesus' presence they would continue to know under the tutelage of the Spirit. Just as Jesus is divine, the Spirit is as well.

The early church recognized and accepted this truth. Early in the book of Acts, the followers of Jesus have gathered as a community characterized by generosity. Many are selling large-ticket items (even parcels of land) and donating the proceeds to the church treasury to be distributed to the needy. In 5:1–11 we learn of a couple, Ananias and Sapphira, who sell a piece of property and bring a portion of the total amount to the apostles. However, they declare publicly that they have brought the full amount. Peter, supernaturally inspired, exposes the charade. The evil, as he makes clear, is not that they kept back part of the proceeds for themselves, but that they attempted to deceive God and his people as to the level of their generosity. Peter's rebuke is particularly instructive as to the full divinity of the Holy Spirit: "Ananias," Peter asked, "why has Satan filled your heart to lie to the Holy Spirit. . . ? How is it that you have contrived this deed in your heart? You did not lie to us but to God!" (Acts 5:3–4). We see here not only Peter's assumption that the Spirit is a personal, conscious agent (one cannot lie to inanimate objects or impersonal life forms), but also through simple parallelism that the Spirit in verse 3 is identified with God in verse 4.

Such scriptural passages led the early church to wrestle with the strict monotheism of the Old Testament. For Israel, the rallying cry of her worship had always been the Shema, found in Deuteronomy 6:4—"Hear, O Israel, the LORD our God, the LORD is one." Now, as a result of the appearance and teaching of Jesus, his followers were compelled both through experience and theological reasoning to recognize as God not just the one Jesus called Father, but also Jesus himself and the Holy Spirit. Yet all three remained distinct from one another as separate persons. How then could Christians hold these three each to be fully divine and yet remain faithful to the monotheism of the Old Testament?

The doctrine of the Trinity arose from the settled conviction that the Father is God, the Son is God and the Holy Spirit is God, together with the settled conviction from the Hebrew Scriptures that there is only one God. The blending of these two convictions led the church over its first three hundred years of theological development to the conclusion that God exists as a unity in diversity: one essence eternally existing as three persons, all sharing equally the divine nature. "Trinity" is the name we use to convey this understanding of God's identity.

Since all three persons of the Trinity share equally the same divine essence and attributes (for example, they are coeternal, infinite in power, knowledge, wisdom, love and glory), what is it that makes them unique from one another? The answer lies in their relation with one another. It is fairly easy for us to grasp something of the relationship between the first and second persons (Father and Son). The Father has begotten the Son from all eternity; the Son is eternally begotten of the Father. The term "begotten" is crucial, because it underscores that the Son was not created by the Father—with regard to the infinite divide between God's nature and the created order, the Son stands eternally on the divine side of the chasm. To create is to make something different from you; to beget is to bring into being something of the same nature as you. So the term "begotten" is critical. But by itself it is not enough. As time-bound creatures we always associate begetting with a time line—the begetter exists and then at some point begets another. In our experience there is always a time when the begotten does not yet exist, but comes into being by the work of a preexisting begetter. It takes a man and a woman, already existing, to join in the process of begetting and birthing a baby, who bears their human nature. Were this to be true of God the Son, we would be forced to conclude, "There was (a time) when he was not," and if so, he could not be called coeternal with God. To help free our thinking from bondage to time concerning the relationship between Father and Son, we confess in the Nicene Creed:

> We believe in one Lord, Jesus Christ,
>   the only Son of God,
>   eternally begotten of the Father. . . .

As long as the Father has existed (from eternity), the Son also has existed. There never was "a time" when he was not. The two have always existed together, and the familial terms "Father" and "Son" indicate their relationship to be one of deep intimacy. With boundless passion God the Father has loved his Son from all eternity; with the same boundless passion God the Son has exulted in his Father for all eternity.

But where does the Holy Spirit fit in all this? We must admit at this point that we are skating on thin ice, having very little of substance from the Scriptures to stand on. Many theologians, particularly in the Orthodox Church traditions of the East, citing Jesus' statement in John 15:26 ("the Spirit of truth, who proceeds from the Father"), have argued that as the Son is eternally begotten by the Father, so the Spirit eternally proceeds from the Father. Unfortunately, this does not dispel the mists much, and it leaves us wondering about the eternal relationship between the Son and the Spirit. In the fourth century Augustine, a North African theologian of great repute, argued for what became known as the "double procession" of the Spirit. Not only the Father, but also the Son, is involved in the eternal generation of the third member of the Trinity. Augustine's view was based more on philosophical insights than biblical data (given the paucity of the latter). He argued that God's essential activity consists of two realities: thinking and willing. "Thinking" he associated with the begetting of the Son (who is the Word of God); "willing" he linked with the procession of the Spirit. It is possible to think without willing, but not to will without thinking. Hence for action to be present, thought must be present. There must be the thinker (the Father) and the thought (the Son) for the willing (the Spirit) to exist. For Augustine then (and the bulk of the Western church since then), the Holy Spirit proceeds from both the first and second members of the Trinity. The Eastern Orthodox have never embraced the "double procession" view, and this remains a theological point of contention between two great traditions of Christian faith.

In the Western church, some theologians have refined the idea of double procession in light of the love relationship between the Father and the Son. We often use the word "spirit" to describe the atmosphere of groups where there is a strong sense of camaraderie (hometown fans at a sporting event) or purpose (members of a long-standing team seeking to reach a coveted goal). While no one argues that this "spirit" is something that exists in itself, we recognize it as an effect of the passionate bond shared by the group. On the divine level, however, the reality of the love shared between the Father and Son is so substantive and vital that what springs forth between them is not merely a shared feeling of unity, but a dynamic, living reality who is the embodiment of the Father and the Son's shared passion. This living person of love we know as the Holy Spirit, whose life proceeds from the Father and the Son.

Granted, such an explanation is quite speculative. After all, we are probing at the edges of the deepest of mysteries. Yet this view holds great attraction because it highlights in a Trinitarian way what the Bible says is most fundamentally true at the divine level: God is love. And any conjecture on Trinitarian interrelationships that highlights love will presumably not be very far off the mark.

3

Getting Tuned In

I have a favorite radio station in Chicagoland. Whenever I am in my Jeep, and the radio is on, it is playing "my music." Every once in a while, after my wife has been behind the wheel, or one of the kids has been fiddling with the dashboard, I climb in the driver's seat only to find the radio tuned to some inferior offering. Not to worry. Through the wonders of technology, I have preprogrammed my station's frequency on memory button number one to return to the tunes that were meant to be. Even if my tastes wander from time to time, I know that all I have to do is hit button number one, and I will be back to "my music." No static, no searching, no worry about hearing the wrong thing.

It is nice to be able quickly and accurately to lock in on something so insubstantial as a radio frequency. Before the days of push-buttons and electronic tuning, manual knobs meant one had to wade through a lot of silence and static before homing in on the desired station. Now memory button number one just snatches the right signals out of the ether, and the receiver distills them into clear and beautiful music.

If experience of the Holy Spirit before the time of Jesus may be likened to the diffuse, often static-filled reception of music on old radio sets, then Jesus may be likened to my memory button number one. As we have already seen, Israel's experience of the Spirit before the time of Christ was rather patchy and vague. While hints existed concerning the Spirit's nature and mission, there was little depth and clarity.

The music of heaven could be heard now and then, sometimes clearly in loud and spectacular bursts, sometimes in soft and gentle phrases, but mostly under conditions of intermittent static and silence. For the four hundred years prior to Jesus' birth, Israel had experienced heaven's static and silence. No prophets, no voice from heaven, no divine intervention.

Then came a man who claimed that the music was about to begin again, but at a whole new level: no longer in fits and starts, no longer competing with overwhelming static, no longer difficult to tune in. That man, of course, we know as John the Baptist, popularly recognized throughout Israel as the first true prophet of God since Malachi. The music he pointed toward was none other than the Holy Spirit, and the tuner/receiver who would broadcast that music to the world would become known as Jesus Christ. Of him John said, "I have baptized you with water, but he will baptize you with the Holy Spirit" (Mark 1:8). Uniquely in Jesus, the Spirit becomes clearly audible—the crushing silence is over. The New Testament teaches that if we want to discover clearly who the Spirit is, we must turn to Jesus. He is, if you will pardon the analogy, memory button number one, to whom the clear frequency of the Spirit is ever attached. Jesus, in his incarnation, is the sole focus of the Spirit's presence and activity in the world. So, if we want to learn about the Holy Spirit, the best place for us to start is to consider the ways in which he and Jesus related during Jesus' earthly life.

The Gospels make clear that with the onset of Jesus' ministry, the world stands at the threshold of the kingdom of God. The time is fulfilled, said Jesus, and a new order of life under the rule of God begins. Central to the onset and development of this new life is the Holy Spirit, who empowers Jesus to beat back the powers of darkness and reclaim the creation for God. It is no accident that each of the Gospel writers highlights the descent of the Spirit upon Jesus at his baptism, emphasizing that his ensuing "kingdom-building ministry" proceeds under the power and aegis of the Spirit of God. Luke makes this abundantly clear by recounting Jesus' first "church sermon," delivered to the hometown audience of Nazareth gathered for Sabbath service. Jesus begins by reading from the scroll of Isaiah a passage brimming with the hope of God's good intervention in a miserable world:

> The Spirit of the Lord is upon me,
>> because he has anointed me
>>> to bring good news to the poor.
>
> He has sent me to proclaim release to the captives
>> and recovery of sight to the blind,
>>> to let the oppressed go free,
>> to proclaim the year of the Lord's favor.
>
> (Luke 4:18–19)

This was widely regarded as a messianic text, that is, a prophetic passage asserting the future anointing of some individual or group (the Messiah) that would restore God's justice and kindness to a topsy-turvy world. For hundreds of years, the Jews had lived with this hope-filled text. Now, in his inaugural sermon in a small Galilean village, Jesus announces, "Today this scripture has been fulfilled in your hearing" (Luke 4:21).

The Hebrew term for "messiah" means literally "the anointed one," and dates back at least to the time of Israel's kings, perhaps even to David himself, where it referred to one who was anointed by God to govern the nation of Israel. By the time of the post-Davidic prophets, it came to have a special meaning beyond this, bundling together Israel's ultimate hopes for the future in the figure of a rescuer/savior uniquely anointed by God. And if God was the anointer of this messiah, the Spirit of God was the "stuff" with which he was anointed. Hence the Isaiah passage, "The Spirit of the Lord is upon me. . . ."

The Gospel writers Matthew and Luke trace the Spirit's relationship to Jesus back to the beginning of his earthly life, making clear that Jesus is from the very beginning the perfect exemplar of human life lived in the atmosphere of the Spirit. His very conception is the work of the Spirit in a young, chaste Jewish girl named Mary. Matthew hints that as the *ruach* (or in Greek the *pneuma*) of God enlivened the first Adam, breathing into him the breath of life, so that same *ruach/pneuma* of God enlivens in a new way the last Adam (see Romans 5 and 1 Corinthians 15 for the apostle Paul's instructive comparison of Adam and Christ). Luke further high-lights the activity of the Spirit surrounding Mary's conception and delivery of the Son of God with a fresh outbreak of prophecy con-cerning Jesus' imminent birth and ultimate mission. This under-scores a favorite theme of Luke, that the Holy Spirit both choreographs and empowers all that Jesus undertakes in his life and ministry.

We see this most clearly during Jesus' baptism in the words spo-ken by the Father as the Spirit rests on Jesus in the form of a dove: "You are my Son, the Beloved; with you I am well pleased" (Luke 3:22). Scholars have long noted that these tandem declarations find Old Testament parallels in Psalm 2, where the divine sonship of the Messiah-King is affirmed, and Isaiah 42:1–4, where God shows his delight in the Servant of the Lord. These two strands of thought become primary in the public ministry that Jesus will exer-cise through the power of the Spirit. As the unique bearer of the Holy Spirit,[2] Jesus wields peerless authority in unfolding the king-dom of God, and yet he exercises that kingly authority as the Suf-fering Servant, whose ultimate sacrifice brings life to the world. Throughout his ministry, Jesus lives in full dependence on his Father, who through the Spirit equips him for this work.

Nowhere is this dependence and equipping more clearly seen than in the wilderness temptations Jesus faces immediately after his baptism. Luke records that Jesus is led out into the desert by the Spirit, where after forty days of fasting he is tempted by the devil to unilaterally meet his own physical needs (turning stones into bread), to take a shortcut to glory (bowing before Satan in order to receive the world from his hands), and to presume upon the Father's care for him because of his unique status as the Son of God (throwing himself from the pinnacle of the Temple to test his Father's attentiveness). It is often thought that Jesus must be at his weakest here as he faces these temptations under the extremes of hunger, silence and loneliness. That is true in one sense. Jesus is at the limit of his natural human resources. But in another sense, he is most clearly dependent on the Spirit of God as he lays aside for forty days every lesser source of strength available so as to rely fully on the strength of the Spirit. Jesus' time apart in the wilderness was a time of spiritual strengthening, not weakening, as he practiced what have always been known to God's people to be spiritual disciplines—fasting, solitude, meditation[3]—in order to draw upon the reserves of heaven for his upcoming battle. In overcoming the enemy's very real attempts to derail his mission, Jesus demonstrates both what human life in full dependence on God looks like and what such a life can accomplish.

It is this continued, unbroken dependence on the Spirit of God that authorizes and enables the fully human Jesus to wield supernatural power for the sake of God's kingdom. The "churchgoers" of his day recognized with excitement that Jesus brought some new power to the table—"With authority he commands even the unclean spirits, and they obey him!" (Mark 1:27). But what they failed to recognize was his total dependence on his Father, the source of the gift of the Spirit enabling Jesus to accomplish what God had sent him to do.

In a profound way, Jesus is the unique bearer of the Holy Spirit, for he alone has lived in full dependence on the Father, or to use other language, without sin. The outpouring of the Spirit upon him enables Jesus to complete his mission as conquering king and suffering servant by traveling the road of the cross for the benefit of humankind. But his earthly life also displays what God's intention is for all human life—what kind of people we can become when we live in full dependence on the Father.

Hence the Gospel writers, particularly Luke and John, portray Jesus not just as the full bearer of the Spirit but the exclusive dispenser of the Spirit to the rest of humanity. John the Baptist's prophetic vision comes true: "He will baptize you with the Holy Spirit," that is, he will cause you to be immersed in the Spirit, filled with his presence, born into a new kind of life and empowered for a new destiny. Though the Spirit is still firmly wedded to Jesus, after his resurrection the Spirit becomes personally available to all who are "in Christ," to all who give Jesus their full allegiance. Prior to the cross, the Spirit remains exclusively with Jesus, but after Christ's atonement for the world, the promises of God are fulfilled in the outpouring of the Spirit upon humanity beginning at Pentecost.[4] The Gospel of John makes clear that this full gift of the

Spirit to humanity is only possible because of Jesus' sacrificial death: "The Spirit had not been given, because Jesus was not yet glorified" (John 7:39). John says this in the context of Jesus' open invitation on the last day of the great Feast of Tabernacles, "If any one thirst, let him come to me and drink. He who believes in me, as the scripture has said, 'Out of his heart shall flow rivers of living water.' " "Living water" is a reference to the Holy Spirit, as John states clearly in 7:38–39. Jesus is the sole dispenser of the Holy Spirit, which he grants freely to any who will come to him in faith. But this promise awaits fulfillment until after Jesus' death, perhaps to make clear to the world that this greatest gift to human beings, the very presence of God within the human heart,[5] is available only because of the mission accomplished by Jesus, the sacrifice of his life for the reclamation of the spiritually dead. When Jesus is glorified (in John's Gospel this is a reference to his crucifixion and subsequent resurrection), then the Spirit can be granted to others. Though John himself does not record the event of Pentecost (it goes beyond the scope of his work), he does relate a postresurrection encounter the disciples have with Jesus that makes clear this truth that the Spirit is now fully available to Jesus' followers, and is given to them by none other than Jesus himself:

> On the evening of that day, the first day of the week, the doors being shut where the disciples were, for fear of the Jews, Jesus came and stood among them and said to them, "Peace be with you." When he had said this, he showed them his hands and his side. Then the disciples were glad when they saw the Lord. Jesus said to them again, "Peace be with you. As the Father has sent me, even so I send you." And when he had said this, he breathed on them, and said to them, "Receive the Holy Spirit." (John 20:19–22)

Evoking the imagery of Spirit as breath, and through the intimacy of breathing upon them, Jesus displays both the close union between himself and the Spirit (breather to breath) and the fact that he dispenses the Spirit to his followers.

So from the time of Jesus' incarnation onward, the Spirit is always tied indissolubly to the person of Jesus. His goal is to make the presence of Jesus universal, and as such he is clothed with the character and personality of Jesus. Whereas prior to the life of Jesus the Spirit was a rather mysterious and undefined figure, now he becomes visible in the hues and brushstrokes of Jesus' life to such an extent that he can be spoken of within the early church as "the Spirit of Jesus" (Acts 16:7), or "the Spirit of Jesus Christ" (Phil. 1:19). Through his activity, the life of Jesus is instantaneously made available to human beings wherever they find themselves and whatever their circumstances, for the Spirit is not bound by space and time, as was the incarnate Jesus.

Perhaps another analogy may help. Suppose that many years ago, friends told you of a particular bed and breakfast in another country that you just had to visit someday. Its name still sits scribbled on the back of a business card in your wallet. Unfortunately, no opportunities ever presented themselves to see firsthand this bit of paradise and find out more about its benefits. Now, however, due to the latest Internet technology, in ten minutes' time you are able to locate the bed and breakfast's website, download a video tour, learn of the owners and even make contact with them through instant messaging. As a result, you find yourself now booking a reservation for you and your spouse to enjoy a rejuvenating week in the European Alps—all because you were able to make an enchanting connection with a place that was otherwise inaccessible to you.

Obviously, we human beings in the twenty-first century are not able to experience walking with the incarnate Jesus through Judean olive groves and Galilean town squares, as did his first disciples. How then are we able to know this same Jesus that they did, to be transformed by his friendship and sent by his personal command as ambassadors of hope into a world choking on emptiness? The New Testament answer to this question is the Holy Spirit. He is God's Internet technology, the enchanting connection who makes the incarnate, and now glorified, Jesus accessible to all who desire to become apprentices of the kingdom of God.

This primary work of the Spirit determines his entire agenda. As in Jesus' ministry we see the Son continually directing attention away from himself and toward his Father, the Spirit's mission is to direct attention away from himself and toward Jesus and his kingdom agenda. He desires to bear witness to and glorify Jesus by unpacking the treasures of the Son and laying them before God's children (John 16:14; see also 15:26).

People often ask how they can be sure a message they hear is really from the Spirit of God rather than a preacher's or their own heart's whisperings. While the full answer to this must be a complex combination of factors, one sure-fire test stems from understanding the Spirit's mission in light of his indissoluble link with Jesus. The Spirit will never bring God's people a message that does not line up with the teaching of Jesus that we already have in the Scriptures, nor will he encourage practices and experiences that are inconsistent with the life that Jesus himself lived on earth. Of any teaching or exhortation we are given we may ask the following core questions: Will pursuing this teaching bring glory to the name of Christ? Will it keep the spotlight of my life on Jesus, or turn attention to me/others?

While it is a common danger of mainline-church Christians to emphasize the Father or the Son in their church experiences and exclude the Spirit through ignorance or anxiety, there are other wings of the church that fall into the opposite error. Pentecostals and charismatics often shift the Trinitarian balance so far in the direction of "experiencing the Spirit" that they almost disconnect the life of the Spirit from the person of Jesus. It is a salutary reminder that the Father intends us to experience and grow in the life of the Spirit, and that this Spirit always intends us to focus on Jesus. We may say with no apologies that one true mark of possessing the Holy Spirit as individuals or communities is that our eyes remain fixed on Jesus throughout the days of our lives—fixed in such a way that we find ourselves increasingly exhibiting the love and holiness that marked his earthly ministry. The Holy Spirit's initial redemptive work in our lives, then, is to get us tuned in to Jesus. But as we will see in the coming chapters, this is just the beginning of the masterpiece he is planning to choreograph and produce.

4

People of the Spirit

As we have already seen, Jesus promised that after his death and resurrection, the Father would send the Holy Spirit into the lives of those belonging to the Way. What ought life look like if the Holy Spirit—that passionate dance of love between the Father and Son, that one whose presence fully conveys the holy life of God—should graciously invade human beings, those entities uniquely created in the image of God? Fortunately, we are not left simply to our imaginations in answering this, because God indeed honored the promise of Jesus fifty days after his crucifixion (during the Jewish Passover Festival) by pouring out the Holy Spirit upon Jesus' followers who had gathered in Jerusalem awaiting fulfillment of this great promise. It happened on the Jewish feast day of Pentecost. God's gracious act of sending his Spirit into this community brought about the birth of the church. A deeper look at the biblical report of this event and its effects in Acts 2 yields the following seven insights.

1. *The movement of the Holy Spirit is not subject to our timing or control.* Jesus, before his ascension, had told his disciples to wait for "the promise of the Father" in Jerusalem, where "you will be baptized with the Holy Spirit not many days from now" (Acts 1:4, 5). Obediently, his followers, numbering about 120 men and women, remained together "constant in prayer," trusting his promise but unsure of what its fulfillment would mean. Luke tells us in Acts 2:1 that on the day of Pentecost, they were all together in one place when

the Holy Spirit suddenly manifested himself through the sounds of violent, rushing wind and the visions of leaping tongues like fire resting on each of them. As we have seen, both wind and fire are vibrant symbols of the Spirit of God in the Old Testament, primarily because they project a sense of fluid mystery and uncontrollable power. Here, as the Spirit invades this upper room, the disciples are filled with his presence in ways they could never have predicted, and the fledgling community is set on a new course, destined in spite of themselves to radically impact the world with new God-given abilities that far exceed their expectations.

2. *The Spirit is given equally to men and women.* This is highlighted not only in Luke's report of Pentecost, when a visible sign of the Spirit (tongue as of fire) rested on *each* of them and *all* of them were filled with the Holy Spirit (2:3, 4), but also in Peter's quotation of the prophet Joel at the beginning of his famous "Pentecost sermon":

> In the last days it will be, God declares,
> that I will pour out my Spirit upon all flesh,
>   and your sons and your daughters shall prophesy,
> and your young men shall see visions,
>   and your old men shall dream dreams.
> Even upon my slaves, both men and women,
>   in those days I will pour out my Spirit;
>   and they shall prophesy.
>
> (Acts 2:17–18)

This compelling fact, above all others, leads to Paul's revolutionary declaration in his letter to the Galatians (3:28), "There is no longer Jew or Greek, there is no longer slave or free, there is no longer male and female; for all of you are one in Christ Jesus."[6]

3. *The gift of the Spirit is a cause for great joy.* What could be of greater fortune than having the divine fount of blessing dwelling at the center of our human community? On that momentous Pentecost day, Jesus' disciples were filled with the Spirit's life to such a degree that some outside observers accused them of being drunk. No group should be this ecstatic, it was thought—they must be nipping at the bottle. Peter, however, seizes this opportunity to com-

ment on this unrestrained joy as a sign of the outpouring of God's Holy Spirit upon his people, a fulfillment of ancient promises pointing to the kingdom of God coming in new power and fullness. So too today the presence of the Holy Spirit elicits joy in the Christian community as we celebrate our unity, love, hope and purpose in Christ.

4. *The Spirit graces God's people with supernatural gifts.* Though we will look at this truth in some detail later on, the point to be made here is that the coming of the Spirit at Pentecost enabled those early Christians to accomplish things beyond their native abilities. Luke reports that after being filled with the Spirit, Jesus' followers started speaking "in tongues," that is, in languages they had never learned but ones known to the many foreigners (see Acts 2:9–11 for a list of countries represented) who had gathered to rubberneck at the scene of the Spirit's advent. This supernatural gift of communication led many of these foreign Jews to wonder: "Amazed and astonished, they asked, "Are not all these who are speaking Galileans? And how is it that we hear, each of us, in our own native language? . . . in our own languages we hear them speaking about God's deeds of power" (Acts 2:7–8, 11). Peter is further gifted supernaturally to proclaim the message of the gospel in such a way that three thousand listeners respond with repentance and newfound faith in Jesus Christ as their Messiah and Lord. Certainly one of the results of the Spirit's residing in and among the people of God is that we are empowered in previously unimaginable ways to serve the world and glorify God.

5. *The Spirit enlivens the church for the primary work of evangelism.* The book of Acts is a record of how the early church community gave itself away in mission to the world, spreading the gospel wherever believers found openings. Peter is not the only one called to go out into the world and make disciples. Before his ascension, Jesus instructed his followers as to their task: "You will be my witnesses in Jerusalem, in all Judea and Samaria, and to the ends of the earth" (Acts 1:8). But he made clear in the first half of verse 8 that this would only happen after they had been empowered by the Spirit for this work. The Spirit motivates, directs and sends Jesus' disciples according to his sovereign will and wisdom,

while at the same time he prepares the hearts and minds of those he has chosen to hear and respond to the message of truth. Why is it that suddenly after Pentecost three thousand Jews respond to the gospel where before there had primarily been confusion and hardness of heart? Why within a few days, as a result of the healing of a lame man and further preaching of the gospel, do up to five thousand more people give their allegiance to Jesus (Acts 4:4)? Although the texts here are not focused on the Spirit's role in softening people's hearts for positive response to the disciples' message, the context makes clear that the coming of the Holy Spirit at Pentecost is the one new element in the mix that now not only empowers believers to speak the word of God courageously but also breaks up the hardened ground of unbelief. Freeing listeners from their unreasonable biases, he now enables them to receive the truth with repentance and faith. What was true in the first century remains true in the twenty-first century. The church is empowered by the Spirit to speak and live the gospel courageously. But for our mission to be successful, we remain dependent on the Spirit for his softening and convicting work in the lives of those to whom he sends us, and the subsequent life of transformation that he brings to pass among the elect.

Charles Haddon Spurgeon, that powerful, Reformed preacher of nineteenth-century England, told how he was walking one evening in London when a derelict approached him in a drunken stupor, leaned up against a lamppost for support and called to him. "Hey, Mr. Spurgeon," he said, "I'm one of your converts!" The preacher replied, "You must be one of mine—you're certainly not one of the Lord's!" It is the Spirit who calls, who enables, who transforms. We must never confuse his field of work with our own.

6. *Pentecost makes clear that God is on the move to reach the whole world with his love.* Though the initial crowd on that momentous Pentecost day was comprised completely of Jews, they were nonetheless Jews from every region of the Roman Empire. The Feast of Pentecost was one of Israel's three holy seasons mandated by God. Every male Jew of age was expected to come to Jerusalem to keep these festivals annually. While in practice this was not possible for all Jews scattered throughout the

world, nevertheless every year thousands of "foreign" Jews[7] would enthusiastically return to their spiritual homeland at these times to offer their prescribed worship. The population of Jerusalem would swell to several times its usual size, and be filled with "every language under heaven" as these diaspora Jews sought to communicate with one another. We know that the common language of the Jews of Judea and Galilee was Aramaic, and that the lingua franca of the Roman Empire was common (Koine) Greek, but most of the foreign Jews would not have known Aramaic, and for most all Jews (hellenized or Palestinian), Greek would be a second language rather than their native tongue.

Those of us who have traveled or lived for extensive periods in a foreign country know the thrill of hearing unexpectedly our own native tongue being spoken. Even though we may be comfortable with our host country's language, to come across someone who speaks our mother tongue is like reaching an oasis after an arduous march through the desert. Our ears zero in like radar dishes till we pinpoint the source, and if possible we strike up a conversation with the person(s) involved. There is something comforting in being reminded of home, and of communicating once again in the language in which we were raised. Though on foreign soil, for a few moments we feel transported home, and sense an immediate kinship with these new acquaintances who share our mother tongue.

It is not hard, then, for us to sense the electricity in the air as the miracle of Pentecost unfolds before the eyes of this diverse crowd of Jews. At first bewildered, because the disciples were mainly Galileans and hence typically unschooled in foreign languages, the onlookers' emotions turn quickly to amazement and wonder as they tune in to the message spoken in their varied mother tongues. Perplexed and thrilled at the same time, they turn to one another and ask, "What does this mean?"

It means one thing at least. God is eager to communicate the good news of his love in Jesus Christ to the world, and to do this he leaps over language barriers to get the message across in the native languages of his listeners. Rather than demand that we learn to decipher the language of heaven, God condescends to the weakness of humanity and translates his truth into the many languages of the world.

In this way, he reverses through his Son the divine curse pronounced at the tower of Babel back at the dawn of civilization. There on the plains of Shinar in the city of Babel, when human beings were flush with the hallucinogen of arrogance and equipped with the powerful tool of a shared mother tongue, we cast off any pretense of needing God, and dreamt of storming the walls of heaven by building a tower high enough to "make a name *for ourselves*" (see Gen. 11:1–9). God stepped in to confound this misguided dream lest human beings think that if we work hard enough together we can by our own ingenuity and muscle achieve the future for which we were created. By splintering human communication into many languages, God averted the prospect of a triumphant humanity, smugly secure in its self-adulation, still as much in need of God's grace as ever, but hopelessly blind to its plight.

In the creation of the church at Pentecost, God undoes the curse of Babel on his own terms, not by giving humanity once again a sole mother tongue, but by enabling peoples of every tribe and tongue to hear his message of salvation in their own home languages. By empowering the disciples to speak beyond language barriers, the Holy Spirit trumpets the Trinity's intent to "get the message out" to all the world.

Unfortunately, but not surprisingly, it took the first disciples a while to understand and embrace God's missionary heart. Unfortunate, because their natural tendency was to think that the message of grace was just for them and their "kind." Not surprising, because the church today often suffers from the same inwardness and exclusivity. However, when God's people yield to the Spirit of Pentecost, we become by his grace not only a warm, welcoming place for all who seek refuge from evil in Christ, but a people on the move, taking the gospel to those like us and those unlike us, to the harassed and helpless near and far. We become a missional people, because we are filled with a missional Spirit, and serve a missional God.

This has tremendous implications for the programmatic life of the church. If we exist not to serve ourselves but the world around us, then our ministries had better reflect that. If our message is meant not for the inner circles but the far corners, then we had better get our feet moving to where there is little or no witness to Jesus Christ. Rather than create multiple congregational programs that coddle members by improving their lives with aerobics workouts, pottery classes and calligraphy lessons, we need to ask ourselves how our self-directed ministries are training us for the mission for which Christ died and rose, for which the Father elected us, for which the Holy Spirit invested himself in us. All our activities and allocation of resources should be measured by the criterion, "How will this help us (me) more faithfully serve the cause of Christ, made clear in the gospel, sealed by the Spirit's action at Pentecost?" Jesus intended his church to be a force on the move forward against evil, not a fortress simply trying to resist the enemy.[8] The Spirit moves us to redemptive engagement with the world, not defensive disengagement.

7. *The Spirit creates a new community recapitulating the life of Jesus Christ.* Though the disciples are already a gathered community in some sense prior to Pentecost, their common life is galvanized in startling ways when the Spirit comes to indwell them. Their lives are bound together with an organic unity, and they find themselves spending as much time together as possible pursuing their joint mission. At the end of Acts 2 we are told concerning the new believers,

> They devoted themselves to the apostles' teaching and fellowship, to the breaking of bread and the prayers.
>
> Awe came upon everyone, because many wonders and signs were being done by the apostles. All who believed were together and had all things in common; they would sell their possessions and goods and distribute the proceeds to all, as any had need. Day by day, as they spent much time together in the temple, they broke bread at home and ate their food with glad and generous hearts, praising God and having the goodwill of all the people. And day by day the Lord added to their number those who were being saved.

Not just as individuals but in their community life as well the early Christians bore witness to the reality of resurrection life in their midst. Through tangible acts of sacrifice they took care of one another; with heartfelt devotion they gathered together around the teaching of the apostles; in groups they worshiped together at the Temple and fellowshiped around the table in common meals. No doubt this unified witness of resolute love played a large part in the rapid growth of the church as outsiders caught glimpses of what genuine human community was always meant to be.

Over the last two thousand years, many visionary dreamers have read the story of the early church and sought to re-create that level of community by requiring followers to give up all personal possessions for the sake of the collective group. Karl Marx is a notable example of this good intent among secular thinkers. However, what all such attempts fail to consider is that this behavioral pattern among the early Christians of Judea was not some program imposed on them by regulation but a voluntary movement inspired by the Holy Spirit, born out of the sacrificial love of Christ for others. It would be wrong for churches today to mandate such sacrifice in order for followers to truly belong. Right motivation cannot be coerced from without; it can only come through the transforming work of the Spirit.

Nevertheless, it is fair to say that the maturity of a Christian congregation can be measured in large degree by the liberal generosity of its members to those in need. Indeed, in this day of scrambling for self-satiation even in the church, where members are looking for what we can "get out of a worship service" or how we can "benefit from a closer walk with God," our pulpits must instead trumpet the truth that the great mark of Christian maturity is found not in how often we feel filled with blessing but rather in how often we allow ourselves to be emptied for others. Where this occurs with regularity, one may be sure that the winds of the Spirit are blowing freely.

The outpouring of the Holy Spirit at Pentecost set in motion a new reality—a people inhabited individually and corporately by the transforming presence of God. The church exists only because God has willed it. It can function by God's will only because the Spirit enlivens and gives purpose to it. One way for us to better understand the work of the Spirit in and among the people of God is to spell out the central marks of the true church, and then seek to discern the role of the Spirit in these arenas.

Most theologians prior to the Reformation agreed that the church is true when characterized by four realities: unity, holiness, catholicity (universality) and apostolicity. To this the Reformers added: the right preaching of the Word of God and the proper administration of the sacraments. Where is the Holy Spirit at work in establishing and maintaining these marks?

Unity. The church is by nature one. Paul's favorite illustration to express this is the human body. To the Corinthian believers he writes:

> For just as the body is one and has many members, and all the members of the body, though many, are one body, so it is with Christ. For in the one Spirit we were all baptized into one body—Jews or Greeks, slaves or free—and we were all made to drink of one Spirit.
>
> Indeed, the body does not consist of one member but of many. If the foot would say, "Because I am not a hand, I do not belong to the body," that would not make it any less a part of the body. . . . Now you are the body of Christ and individually members of it. (1 Cor. 12:12–15, 27)

Paul makes clear that the agency of this unity is the one Spirit of God, who immerses all believers into the common life of Jesus Christ. This supernatural unity achieved by the hand of God in uniting us to Jesus Christ reaches deeper than any differences that may threaten to divide us, for now because of the Spirit we find our core identity in Jesus Christ, and anyone else who claims this same core identity becomes our sister or brother in Christ. No longer do formerly crucial distinctives retain first place in our self-descriptions, whether they be race, ethnicity, gender, social class, even denomination. For example, I am not an Arab American, suburban, middle-class, Presbyterian man who happens to be a Christian, but rather a human being belonging to Christ—who happens to be of Arab background, male and Presbyterian. When I meet another believer in Christ, she is my sister and we share a profound kinship, even though she happens to be an African American, inner-city Baptist.

Those distinctives that apart from Christ would have polarized us have now in Christ become qualities that can enrich our shared life, for we find our joint identities in the same Lord and Savior.

That is why Paul can exult, "In Christ there is no longer Jew or Greek, slave or free, male or female"—he who unites us is greater than that which would polarize us. Likewise, as Paul exhorts the Ephesians to maintain the gift of the unity of the Spirit in the bond of peace (4:3), he supports that by arguing: "There is one body and one Spirit, just as you were called to the one hope of your calling, one Lord, one faith, one baptism, one God and Father of all, who is above all and through all and in all " (4:4–6). The one Spirit who unites us to the one body of Christ not only creates a new unity available nowhere else and in no other way, but also he maintains us in this unity, for he is our sole and indispensable connector to the living Christ.

Holiness. In Leviticus 19:2 God declares through Moses to the people of Israel, "You shall be holy, for I the LORD your God am holy." It should come as no surprise to us that the agent who brings to pass this divine intention is none other than the *Holy* Spirit. What does it mean, though, in practical terms to say that the true church is marked by holiness?

For many in today's culture, the term "holiness" smacks of sanctimony or privatized pietism—either a parade of long-nosed pharisaical judgments or a retreat from active engagement with the real world to pursue personal moral agendas. Yet since Leviticus 19 demands that our holiness is to be of the same character and quality as God's, such views must be rejected as perversions of God's intent. Instead, we discover throughout Scripture that the biblical concept is positive and engaging. The root imagery behind holiness is the action of being set apart from the ordinary, or to use another biblical phrase, "being sanctified." Biblical writers apply it to objects as well as to people. For example, in Jewish Temple life, many utensils were needed to carry out the various rites and sacrifices commanded by God. Many of these same types of utensils (e.g., lavers, knives, plates) were used in ordinary life as well. To be employed in Temple service, however, required that they be "sanctified" or set apart for this holy usage. Once placed in this unique service, they were never to be utilized in an ordinary (pro-fane) way again. In the church we see this same principle at work, particularly when it comes to the elements involved in the sacra-ment of *Holy* Communion. The bread and wine are "set apart from their common and ordinary use to this most holy and sacred use" (adapted from the Second Helvetic Confession, *Book of Confes-sions* 5.178). Such holiness is always borrowed; that is, it derives its meaning and power from being rightly related to God's pur-poses and desires.

Yet in the New Testament the idea of holiness is most often associated with people in relationship to God, and that also is a borrowed reality. To be holy, in this sense, is to be set apart by God from our self-determined or societally cast agendas in order to become fully available to God for his kingdom purposes.[9] The church is holy, then, as it relinquishes any pretensions to pursuing its own goals, no matter how laudable they may seem, and yields itself to the vision for which God has set it apart.

But there is another sense to holiness in the Bible as well, and this has much to do with that vision. To be a holy people in this second sense is to be a community on a journey toward moral wholeness, concerned with living authentic human lives, reflect-ing with increasing virtue what it means to be created in the image of God. Paul typically casts this vision in terms of conformity to the likeness of Jesus, the only truly human person who provides our model. So together, by God's grace, we are to grow "until all of us come to the unity of the faith and of the knowledge of the Son of God, to maturity, to the measure of the full stature of Christ" (Eph. 4:13). Holiness is never envisioned as a private matter in the Scriptures, though it demands wholehearted personal commit-ment. At its core it is relational, and based on the two central com-mands of Scripture, that we love God with every fiber of our being, and that we love our neighbors as ourselves.

This journey of holiness, if it is ever to be more than an exter-nal act or conformity to rules, requires the transforming work of the Holy Spirit, who alone can take hearts of flinty stone and turn them into hearts of warm flesh. This is the central and defining feature of the new covenant that God has made with humanity in

Christ—that his law will no longer simply be written on stone, and its attainment left to inadequate human efforts, but now with the advent of the Holy Spirit, that same law will be written on human hearts, and its fulfillment enabled by the new life of the Spirit. We belong to a new covenant, says Paul, "not in a written code but in the Spirit; for the written code kills, but the Spirit gives life" (2 Cor. 3:6). As a result of this new covenant relationship with God, we are the focus of the Spirit's sanctifying work, which brings us closer and closer to perfection in Christ. Or again in the words of Paul, "And we all, with unveiled face, beholding the glory of the Lord, are being changed into his likeness from one degree of glory to another; for this comes from the Lord who is the Spirit" (2 Cor. 3:18).

Catholicity. When, as Reformed Christians, we say in the Apostles' Creed, "We believe in the holy catholic church," we are not referring specifically to the Roman Catholic Church, though that branch of the church has a venerable tradition. The term "catholic" as intended in the creed means "universal" and is closely aligned with the sense of the oneness of the church. While the mark of unity emphasizes our identity in Christ, however, the mark of catholicity speaks of the fact that there is only one avenue of salvation for any and all people. From the time of Adam until the second coming of Christ there is only one people of God—those saved by the grace of God now made known fully in the gospel of Jesus Christ and appropriated by faith.

In Romans 4 Paul uses Abraham's relationship with God as a model of how we are made right with God, whether Jew or Gentile, whether raised under the divine law or in ignorance of it. Though he lived centuries before the giving of the law and almost two thousand years before the coming of Christ, Abraham was declared righteous by God because he placed his trust in God's gracious promises rather than trusting in his own plans for the future. According to Paul, Abraham's lifestyle of trust in the God who keeps his gracious word is the proper model for all human beings. There are no exceptions to this process of being made right with God. There are no other paths sanctioned by God but dependence on his mercy made known consummately in Jesus Christ, "in him every one of God's promises is a 'Yes'" (2 Cor. 1:20). To say the church is catholic, therefore, is to declare that there is only one way to God, through Jesus Christ, and that this way is open to all people of every time and every place. The church, comprised of all those saved by the gracious activity of the one true God, reflects that there is only one avenue of salvation. There are no rival peoples of God, who reach the halls of heaven in some other way than through trust in the work of God on our behalf. In this sense, we can embrace the theological statement, "There is no salvation outside the church," because we recognize the church to comprise all who come to God by faith through Jesus Christ. The church is catholic or universal because there are no other means to salvation than the gospel of Jesus Christ.

How is the Holy Spirit involved in this arena? According to Scripture and Reformed theology, human beings by nature are spiritually "dead in their sins and trespasses," and therefore deaf to God's appeals to turn toward him. Indeed, many today have no sense that they need to be reconciled to God, that their choices and intentions have left them under the wrath of a just God. On his deathbed Henry David Thoreau was asked by his sister if he had made his peace with God, and is reported to have answered, "I did not know that we had argued." Whether or not he said this, the sentiment expresses the view of vast numbers today. How do those who are content in their status without God become responsive to the gospel so as to embrace the mercy of God offered in Jesus Christ?

According to Jesus, this transformation happens only through the ministry of the Holy Spirit, who "will prove the world wrong about sin and righteousness and judgment: about sin, because they do not believe in me; about righteousness, because I am going to the Father and you will see me no longer; about judgment, because the ruler of this world has been condemned" (John 16:8–11). He does this by demonstrating that evil at its core stems from unbelief in Christ, that the only human hope for righteousness lies in the completed work of Christ, who after his resurrection ascended to the throne beside his Father, and that the way of independence and rebellion has already been condemned at the cross—that way leads to death. These truths remain external to the human heart, until the Holy Spirit removes the blinders of our spiritual smugness and shows us the desperate condition of our own hearts. The veil of illusion remains over our eyes, the hardness of our hearts grows ever more dense until the Spirit of God brings freedom from these conditions caused by sin (2 Cor. 3:14–17). Once we are aware of our disorder and the cure that God has made available in Christ, we are guided to response by the Spirit, who leads us through the narrow gate that leads to life. Then together with Peter and the rest of the confessing church, we say concerning Jesus Christ, "There is salvation in no one else, for there is no other name under heaven given among mortals by which we must be saved" (Acts 4:12).

Apostolicity. The church can truly be one, holy and catholic only as it is also apostolic. But this refers not in the first instance to the "original apostles." Instead, it points back to God himself, whose nature is apostolic. This strange-looking English term is a loanword from the Greek language, based on a verb that means simply "to send." To be an apostle is to be one sent as a messenger to another. In this sense, God the Son in his incarnation became the preeminent apostle to the world, and the Holy Spirit, sent from both the Father and the Son, carries on this unique apostolic ministry to the church and world. The church is apostolic first and foremost because it is built upon receiving what the Father has sent to the world, and second because now in his name it is sent forth on the wings of the Spirit with his message of good news for the world. According to the Great Commission of Matthew 28:19–20, Jesus commanded his followers to go out into the world to make disciples; but as we have seen in the story of Pentecost, before he sent them out into the world, he sent the Spirit into them. This empowering is just as necessary for the church today as it was in the first century. The Holy Spirit demonstrates through his ministry of presence God's desire to reach the whole world with his love. This missionary heart, expressed through the sending of his Son into the world and the consequent gift of the Spirit to enliven his people to be a light for the world, is what makes the church apostolic.

We today build on the foundation of Jesus Christ because of the

Spirit who energized those first apostles to proclaim the message of the gospel beyond their own comfort zones to people of all stripes and colors. The church remains apostolic as we flow with the current of the Holy Spirit, who remains a missionary to the world, pointing lost people in every way and every place to the glory of Jesus Christ.

5

Spirit-Filled Worship?

*I*t is hard to imagine a much better definition for worship than that of Archbishop William Temple, "To worship is to quicken the conscience by the holiness of God, to feed the mind with the truth of God, to purge the imagination by the beauty of God, to open the heart to the love of God and to devote the will to the purpose of God" (in *The Hope of a New World*, London: SCM Press, 1940). Hidden within each of these verbal phrases is the enabling ministry of the Holy Spirit, weaving into our minds, emotions, wills, consciences and imaginations the manifold wonders of God's glory.

Since the 1960s, some Christian circles have adopted the term "Spirit-filled worship" to distinguish their church services from those of other Christian groups. What is meant by such a designation?

For some the phrase seems simply a way of saying, "Our worship is better than your worship," sort of on a par with playground quarrels ending with, "Well, my father can beat up your father." Needless to say, such an approach would belie the description "Spirit-filled." Who can imagine the Spirit of God inspiring some worshipers to belittle what other worshipers are seeking to offer God?

For others, though, the idea of "Spirit-filled worship" brings to mind a style that differs significantly from that found in older, mainline churches. Free of traditional, liturgical trappings, such an approach often jettisons older hymnody in favor of more modern tunes and simpler, emotive lyrics, often called "praise music." The order of worship is typically simple and allows for spontaneity in the flow of events. Depending on how the Spirit moves, the length of service varies, ending when the leadership senses that God is bringing the time to a close.[10] Public messages sometimes come in the form of expository sermons by the preaching pastor or in prophetic utterances by members of the congregation under the inspiration of the Spirit. "Spirit-filled" worship in Pentecostal and charismatic circles is usually characterized by speaking or singing "in tongues" as well as other activities known as "sign gifts,"[11] such as interpretation of tongues, words of knowledge, healings and miracles.

Many younger people are attracted to what is seen as a fresher form of worship than that offered by traditional churches. On the other hand, some traditionalists argue that what happens mostly in "praise worship" is not worship at all but simple pandering to the entertainment urge prevalent in modern society. The worship service becomes structured to appeal to what attracts people musically, visually, socially. But is there not something unique and substantive to Christian worship that should not be sacrificed to the vagaries of passing fad? Does the Holy Spirit need "props" in order to lead people to a life-transfixing encounter with God?

These "worship wars" have been occurring in American churches with increasing frequency over the last four decades. This ought to make us pause. Perhaps the issue is not just style, but substance. Perhaps mainline churches can learn from the unintended critique of "Spirit-filled" churches concerning worship, and vice versa. Indeed, all worship should be "Spirit-filled," but perhaps not quite in the way often assumed.

In reality, there can be no worship of God that is not Spirit-filled, that is, inspired and directed by the Spirit of God. If, as Reformed theology teaches, we are incapable of turning ourselves toward God and under our own steam offering him the worship he truly deserves, then only as the Holy Spirit empowers us can we enter into this arena appropriately. From the start the Spirit must be in charge, or there will be no worship worthy of that name.

What are the necessary elements of such worship? To begin with, we must refresh our understanding of what worship is all about. It is obviously not simply the routine of getting up every

Sunday morning to put in an hour's appearance at church. It is not "an opportunity to network" for social or business reasons. It is not even primarily the time I go "to get fed" or stimulated.

Worship as the Bible portrays it is part of an encounter with the living God, mediated by the wind and fire of his Spirit. The encounter is two-way, with God acting sovereignly on his part, and with us offering him our worship—demonstrating in multiple ways his worth and worthiness. There should be nothing passive about worship, for we gather in the sanctuary to celebrate the one who is beyond equal, for whose description there are not enough superlatives, who has inundated us with love beyond measure and rescued us with unmatched power. As Peter says, we have been set apart "in order that you may proclaim the mighty acts of him who called you out of darkness into his marvelous light" (1 Pet. 2:9).

Worship correctly understood is a kind of performance. But it is our performance, not God's. Søren Kierkegaard was absolutely right in his critique of much that passes for worship in our churches. Many people gather to sit in the pews, waiting for the service to start much in the same way they wait for a play to begin. They look up on the chancel, where they see the principal actors—the professional clergy and musicians. God is there, one hopes, behind the scenes as the prompter, in case one of the actors should forget her lines. The audience in the pews grows quiet as the performance begins, silently hopeful. If all goes well, as the crowds exit they tell the actors how greatly they enjoyed the show, or how much they "got out of it."

But as Kierkegaard pointed out, we've got the parts all wrong. In true worship, we the congregation are not the audience but the actors. The worship leaders are not the actors but the prompters to help the congregation with its "lines." And God is not the prompter but the audience. Worship is the offering of our best devotion to an audience of one.

As such, it is an activity of self-giving rather than of getting. Many of us betray our misunderstanding of, or even worse, our self-centered approach to, worship when we leave the sanctuary saying to one another, "I didn't get much out of that today," or "Why can't we end on time?" as if God exists for our benefit and timetable.

Hence worship inspired by the Spirit is always focused Godward. How could it be any other way when we are under the guidance of the one who always points toward Christ? If we find ourselves attempting to generate a certain kind of feeling with our worship, or to give people a "good worship experience," then it is time to reassess our efforts with the question, Whom are we aiming to please? In the end, this is not an either/or, as long as we keep our priorities straight. If we intend through worship to offer ourselves to God for his pleasure, then we will discover our own pleasure thrown in as a bonus. If, however, we seek to put ourselves first, our worship will never bring God the delight that it ought.

Second, since in worship we encounter the God who is beyond our finite comprehension, Spirit-filled services will always feature a healthy dose of awe-inspiring mystery. By the mediation of the Spirit, the throne room of heaven is brought to our hearts, and our worship gathering is lifted heavenward. Those with eyes to see will marvel at the bigness of God, at his beauty reflected in the elegant balance and order of creation, at his unreachable wisdom that makes foolish the best of mortal wisdom. But even more, they will wonder continually that God should desire to make his home with frail creatures of dust, that he should take a merciful interest in the future of a renegade race, that he should display his glory so freely in Christ to win our allegiance from darkness.

> Tis mercy all, immense and free,
> For, O my God, it found out me.
> Amazing love, how can it be
> That Thou, my God, shouldst die for me![12]

A worship service devoid of wonder is a contradiction in terms. Yet in so many of our churches today, the most precious truths of all are handled like dirty dishes at the local truck stop. The mystery of grace made available for sinners has been lost. Our eyes of faith have been gouged out by the thumbs of routine. In the words of Elizabeth Barrett Browning,

> Earth's crammed with heaven,
> And every common bush afire with God;
> But only he who sees takes off his shoes—
> The rest sit round it and pluck blackberries.[13]

What we need are new eyes to see as if for the first time, but such a miracle can only come from the Spirit of God. The good news is that God is still in the business of miracles, and having already poured out the full measure of his Spirit upon the church, he has promised to grant us what we need and hunger for.

Because of the nature of God in Jesus Christ, true worship is characterized by unpredictability. God is not tamed by our liturgy—bored, maybe, but not tamed. In his sovereign freedom he retains the right to meet us in any way he chooses: the still small voice of Elijah, the whirlwind of Job, the fiery chariots of Ezekiel, the angelic hallelujah chorus of the first Christmas night, the understated conversation of the Emmaus road. Worship inspired by the Spirit recognizes that control of the encounter rests with God, not us, and so there is breathless anticipation in the air. In her book *Teaching a Stone to Talk*, Annie Dillard writes,

> Why do people in churches seem like cheerful, brainless tourists on a packaged tour of the Absolute? . . . Does anyone have the foggiest idea what sort of power we so blithely invoke? . . . [We are like] children playing on the floor with chemistry sets, mixing up a batch of TNT . . . it is madness to wear straw hats or velvet hats to church. We should all be wearing crash helmets. Ushers should issue life preservers and signal flares, they should lash us to our pews . . . for God may draw us out to where we can never return.[14]

C. S. Lewis captures this same truth in the first of his Narnia Chronicles, *The Lion, the Witch, and the Wardrobe,* but adds an important caveat to the unpredictability of God. In this fantasy novel, the four Pevensie children are whisked magically into the kingdom of Narnia, a unique world of talking beasts, over whom Aslan is king. When the children first hear the name of Aslan, they are filled with mysterious feelings ranging from dread to excitement to contentment to yearning. Later, when they are in the home of Mr. and Mrs. Beaver, and the name is mentioned again, the children probe for more information. To the question, "Who is Aslan?" Mr. Beaver responds, "He's the King, the Lord of the whole wood. . . ." When the children discover that the plan is for them to meet Aslan, suddenly they are not so eager. They seek reassurance in the hope that Aslan is at least human, like them:

"Is—is he a man?" asked Lucy.

"Aslan a man!" said Mr. Beaver sternly. "Certainly not. I tell you he is the King of the wood and the son of the great Emperor-Beyond-the-Sea. Don't you know who is the King of the Beasts? Aslan is a lion—*the* Lion, the great Lion."

"Ooh!" said Susan, "I'd thought he was a man. Is he—quite safe? I shall feel rather nervous about meeting a lion."

"That you will, dearie, and no mistake," said Mrs. Beaver, "if there's anyone who can appear before Aslan without their knees knocking, they're either braver than most or else just silly."

"Then he isn't safe?" said Lucy.

"Safe?" said Mr. Beaver. "Don't you hear what Mrs. Beaver tells you? Who said anything about safe? 'Course he isn't safe. But he's good. He's the King, I tell you."[15]

Because of this divine freedom coupled with divine goodness, Spirit-filled worship is characterized by expectation. God indeed will *meet* us in worship, and such a meeting with him is always redemptive.

A few people in my life are so full of love and goodness that I always look forward to being with them. The sky seems bluer, the sun brighter and my spirits are always lifted when I am in their presence. The prospect of spending time together with them invariably makes me impatient for that occasion, kind of like a trail horse that has been ridden all day and now turned toward home and given its head. The anticipation of the goal overpowers all lesser stimuli.

How much more should that be the case with God! To gather with his people where he promises his presence should fill us with a holy expectancy. We gather to worship; God comes to bless us, or rather, his coming is our blessing.

Since the Lord cannot be domesticated yet is good, and since he calls us to gather with expectancy, worship should be character-ized by excitement. When our services reflect a business-as-usual attitude, we can be sure that our hearts or minds, or both, have derailed somewhere. On the other hand, excitement does not necessarily mean jumping up and down, pumping our fists and yelling like Tarzan, as crazed sports fans are wont to do. Excitement is also seen in the keen, riveting stillness that grips a young wife and her children as they spy the navy ship entering port with their husband/father returning from a six-month tour of duty. Excitement is capable of a wide range of behaviors, all of which depend on context for their appropriateness. Worship is no exception. David could dance before the Lord after seeing God mighty in battle. Seekers amid the early Christians could crane their necks as a man lame from birth was healed in their midst. Israel could shout so loudly when the ark of the covenant arrived in their midst that the ground around them reverberated (1 Sam. 4:5). Cleopas and his friend could feel their hearts burn within them as the Scriptures were unfolded before them in ways that exalted their Lord. A worship service that engenders no sense of excitement at coming into God's presence needs to be put out of its misery. Better yet, it begs for a spiritual transfusion.

To bow before the sovereign presence of God is to recognize that we are not in charge of the encounter. Whatever of lasting value transpires comes from his initiative and handiwork. While God has given us clear guidelines as to the essential elements of worship, he is not locked in to following a certain prescribed order. Attempts therefore to tightly control a worship service in terms of what may or may not happen and how long or short its parts should be run the risk of shutting the Spirit out of our gathering for an ordered but empty human endeavor.

This is not to say that the God we worship is a God of confusion. We in the Reformed tradition are particularly fond of Paul's declaration concerning worship that all things should be done decently and in order (1 Cor. 14:40) precisely because God is not a God of confusion but of peace (14:33). But worship guided by the Spirit will find its order and aptness in the leading of God rather than simply in human determination. It is hard for those who have grown up in a culture emphasizing initiative and independence, and who have been trained for traditional church leadership, to hand over the keys to the sanctuary, even to God. If we are not in charge, then we cannot guarantee the outcome. What if God should choose to do something that we do not like? Or to demand more from us than we were thinking of giving? And how can we be sure that we are following the guidance of the Spirit rather than our own private leanings?

Yet the reality portrayed in both Old and New Testaments is that even in the developing liturgy of Temple worship, and later in the move to synagogue gatherings, there was a lot more spontaneity and openness to the choreography of the Spirit than we find in many of our congregations today. Faith in God demands taking risks, even in the context of worship. If we wish to meet with God, we must be ready to come on his terms, ceding our control and private agendas, ready to wait or respond according to his initiative. When we are willing to do this, worship becomes an exciting, unpredictable, yet fulfilling event.

For example, when we expect that God will speak in our midst (as he has promised), the reading and preaching of the Bible come alive with anticipation. Reformed theology speaks of the "inspiration of the Holy Scriptures," by which is meant that the varied human authors were each divinely guided in their efforts in such a way that without squelching their unique perspectives and peculiarities, God effectively communicated his message through their words. Therefore, when we hear the Bible read and proclaimed, we expect that through it we will really encounter the living Word of God, and so experience increasing transformation into his likeness. When this fails to happen on a consistent basis, there has been a disconnect somewhere. Since we recognize that God, who sent his Son to be the incarnate Word for the world, is not slow to communicate with us human beings, the short circuit in the communication process must lie in us. That is why Reformed worship services are characterized by an explicit plea to God for help in clearly hearing what he is saying—we call this the "prayer for illumination," which usually occurs just before the reading of Scripture. Our prayer is that the same Spirit who inspired the texts of the Bible and points unerringly to Christ will free us from our fallen biases that inherently twist the truth to serve our own self-centered ends. Hence the Spirit works in our worship not only to provide us the "God-breathed"[16] Scripture and reveal Jesus Christ in our midst, but to set us free from our preconceptions and ideological lenses so as to hear, receive and respond appropriately to God's transforming truth in Christ. Spirit and Word are forever wedded in the kingdom of God. As Martyn Lloyd-Jones is reputed to have said, "Nothing is more dangerous than to put a wedge between the Word and the Spirit, to emphasize either one at the expense of the other. It is the Spirit *and* the Word, the Spirit *upon* the Word, and the Spirit in us as we read the Word."

The ministry of the Spirit in the life and message preparation of the preacher, as well as in the actual delivery of the sermon, is critical. But equally critical is the ministry of the Spirit in the preparation of worshipers as we listen for God's message to us. In my twenty years of pastoral ministry, one of the practical truths I have discovered is this: those individuals who regularly tell me that I preached "exactly what they needed to hear" are the very same individuals whose lives reflect passionately an openness to and eagerness for the leading of God. The same Spirit who inspires the biblical text illumines the worshipful heart.

The same dynamic is present in our individual and corporate prayers of confession. Reformed theology teaches that true repentance is a divine gift, brought about by the conviction of the Holy Spirit. Worship enlivened by the Spirit's presence creates an atmosphere in which words of penitence often repeated by rote, or scanned with little thought, suddenly flare to life with the fires of guilt and grief. Our consciences accuse us, and our souls bow low in the presence of the Holy One, whispering age-old confessions: "Against you, you alone, have I sinned" (Ps. 51:4); "We have offended you deeply" (Neh. 1:7). By the grace of the Holy Spirit, we feel the darkness of our evil, and as we turn away from it and back toward God we experience the release from our guilt and shame that Christ made possible through his death on the cross. What a gift day in and day out, week in and week out, for human beings to find cleansing for our hideous heart stains and cool relief from the hot winds of shame. Worship in the Spirit deals forthrightly with our sins, and applies the healing oils of grace to our cracked and wounded souls.

The same is true of our participation in the sacraments of baptism and Communion. Apart from the empowering ministry of the Holy Spirit in our lives, our observance of these rites remains mere external performance. Until the capacity of faith is generated in our hearts and minds, we remain impervious to these sacraments as means of grace that lead us into deeper community with Jesus Christ. We may still participate, but we are like the blind whose eyes never capture the sun's rays that shine on them, or the deaf whose eardrums fail to register the sound waves that impinge on them.

When the Spirit enlivens us, however, the sacrament of baptism confirms and seals the fact of our adoption as children of God. We are ingrafted by the Holy Spirit into the life of the only begotten Son so that we are able to participate fully in the relationship that he shares with his Father. So we are reborn from children of the flesh into children of the Spirit. By means of this sacrament, the Spirit links our lives with that of Jesus, so that we embrace his death and resurrection, and hence move from our natural destiny of death to the new destiny of eternal life. Also by means of baptism, the Spirit displays his vocation as the one who unites all things in Christ. By uniting each believer to Christ, he binds us one to another as well. Hence we become members of the body of Christ, no longer estranged from God and one another. Now we belong to one another; as with the human body, what affects one limb or organ has a decided impact on the rest. We live now under the guidance of our one head, Jesus Christ, and the body is enlivened by the eternal presence of his Spirit. Hence we gather regularly as the body of Christ, because we are bonded inseparably to the Son of God and so to one another. The sacrament of baptism, when graced by the Holy Spirit, declares and seals all these realities in the lives both of the community and of the individual.

This same principle undergirds the sacrament of the Lord's Supper. The Spirit's quickening of our hearts in faith enables us to meet Christ in the act of receiving the elements of bread and wine. He applies the rich grace of God to our spiritual needs and thereby nourishes our souls for continued growth in the likeness of Jesus. Both Communion and baptism are celebrations of what the Lord has done and continues to do for his people. Yet they only become personal celebrations as we open ourselves to the unique ministry of the Holy Spirit, who not only points us to Christ in outward ways, but prepares our hearts inwardly to receive him earnestly.

In the final analysis, all true worship is Spirit-filled worship. From a Reformed theological perspective, there can be no other. No doubt this is in part what Jesus meant in his comment to the Samaritan woman at the well that anyone who worships God must do so in spirit and truth (John 4:23–24)—they must approach God the Father within the relationship of the Son as made possible by the Holy Spirit. In this encounter, we come and bow gladly before God, offering the sum total of who we are in humble recognition that he rightly holds the title deed to our lives. But the good news is that God also comes to meet us in this encounter, and he comes with arms full of gifts for his children.

In the next chapter, we discuss the gifts that God freely gives his people. What is important to know as we bring this chapter to a close is that all God's gifts spring from being united to him in Jesus Christ, and this bond is both accomplished and strengthened through "Spirit-filled" worship.

6

The Gift That Keeps on Giving

*M*y good friend Thomas Smoak runs a ministry to street kids in São Paulo, Brazil. I will never forget his story about young Wesley, the son of a drug-addicted prostitute who in her own neediness could not provide a home and so abandoned him. At the age of seven, he came under the care of Abba, Thomas's ministry. Realizing he would never return "home," Wesley began praying to be adopted, an unlikely outcome for a preteen street kid. Though he begged and begged God, for three years nothing seemed to happen. Time and again, his ten-year-old mind and his one-year-old faith gave out in doubt and depression. "I'm not going to pray any more," he would cry. "God doesn't hear me." Then, under the encouragement of the Smoaks and remembering the good promises of God, he would make a fresh start, praying for new parents with urgency, praying with hope, praying with fervency. The Smoaks had no idea where such a couple might materialize, yet did not want to squelch Wesley's frail yearnings.

Unbeknownst to them all, at about the same time Wesley came to Abba, Tim and Jeanette, a middle-aged couple unable to have children of their own, began the Brazilian state adoption process. It took them three years of paperwork and waiting, until they finally decided that due to their age and position in life, they were more suited to be the parents of a ten-year-old than an infant. The Smoaks became aware of this possibility, and Tim and Jeanette began participating in some of Abba's activities with the street children. Meanwhile, Wesley was praying and doubting and trying to believe, as God was working behind the scenes.

"We'll never forget," Thomas says, "the day we went to the judge, and Tim and Jeanette met us there. The lady in the judge's office turned to Wesley and said, 'Wesley, do you know Tim and Jeanette?'

" 'Yeah,' he responded. 'They're the aunt and uncle that take us on *paseos*, and go to the water park with us, and to the zoo, and . . . I love them!'

" 'Well,' she said, 'they want to adopt you.' "

Wesley was silent. He could not believe it. After three and a half years of waiting, this was the best possible couple in the world as far as he was concerned. They made plans right away for their new family life. But Wesley could not go home with them that day. He still had to finish school and some other commitments where he was at Abba, but that day Tim and Jeanette took him for a tour of what would soon become his new home. He saw his new bedroom. Tim gave Wesley the teddy bear he had grown up with and saved for the firstborn son he was never able to have. The couple gave Wesley a wallet-sized picture of themselves, saying, "These are *your* parents now." At the end of the day, when they arrived back at the Abba house, Wesley was asleep, snuggled up against Tim's shoulder. Tim carried him to his bed and tucked him in gently.

The next morning, Wesley woke up still in his old surroundings. He had wet the bed, as he always did; the room smelled the same as it always did; the walls were as dirty as the day before; the floor linoleum was still peeling; the people looking at him were the same, messy street-kid faces that he always saw; he went back that day to the same school; and Tim and Jeanette were not there. But he had a picture in his pocket. He showed it to his teacher and said, "Teacher, I got adopted! These are my mom and dad. These are my parents! They're going to take me to the States; they're going to take me to Disney World! I'm going to learn to speak English! I got adopted, and this is my proof!"

The only thing that had changed in Wesley's world that day was the picture clutched in his hand. But it served as the guarantee that soon everything was going to be different. It was the down payment toward the fulfillment of a new life.

The Holy Spirit is God's picture given to us. He is the guarantee that we belong to Christ, and that all of God's promises will come to fruition for us. He is heaven's escrow account on the future God has sculpted for a redeemed creation. The apostle Paul confirms this by using the language of "first fruits," "seal" and "down payment."

In Romans 8:18ff. Paul directs his readers' attention to the future fulfillment of all God's promises as a means of enduring their present suffering. The hope of the resurrection provides the context for Christ's followers to see life's groanings as labor pains preceding the ultimate unveiling of the new creation rather than as death throes of a tortured and meaningless existence. So he writes: "We know that the whole creation has been groaning in labor pains until now; and not only the creation, but we ourselves, who have the first fruits of the Spirit, groan inwardly while we wait for adoption, the redemption of our bodies. For in hope we were saved. Now hope that is seen is not hope" (Rom. 8:22–24a). The "first fruits[17] of the Spirit" refers to the new life imparted to believers by the Spirit through his ingrafting us into the Son of God. As Paul makes clear in Romans 6–8, this new life has gained a foothold in the lives of Christians, but has not yet completed the process of transforming us from stumbling servants of sin to perfected children of God. The presence of the Spirit in our lives, however, serves as the first fruits of the full harvest that is still to come. His present ministry is a small foretaste of the complete changeover that shall reach its culmination when we stand before Christ at the end of days.

Similar in thought is the idea that God has given his people the Holy Spirit as a down payment on the complete future he has promised. The Greek word used by Paul in 2 Corinthians 1:22, 5:5 and Ephesians 1:14 was originally a commercial term referring to money put forward as a deposit or pledge on the full amount of sale. This earnest money showed the good faith of the interested party, indicating that the full amount would be given at a designated point in the future. Interestingly, this word is still used in modern Greek culture, and bears as one of its meanings the term "engagement ring," which of course is given in pledge of a full love relationship to be consummated in future marriage. This modern usage captures the sense Paul intended regarding God's gift of the Holy Spirit to the church as well as the individual believer in Christ. The current presence of the Spirit is God's guarantee on the future toward which he is aiming, the vision of culmination that hovers at the margins of every page of Scripture. In the words of the NRSV, God has given us "his Spirit in our hearts as a first installment" (2 Cor. 1:22), "the pledge of our inheritance toward redemption as God's own people" (Eph. 1:14).

In a similar vein, Paul views the Holy Spirit as the seal of God's as yet unfulfilled promises in the lives of Christ's followers. In the ancient world, a seal consisted of an official mark (usually made by an imprint upon hot wax) that conveyed that the sealed object was either owned by or under the authority of the one with the seal. The Spirit in this sense becomes the official "mark" upon the individual believer (as well as the entire body of Christ), signifying God's ownership of his people, and his authority to be able to complete what he has begun in Christ.

As the one who makes the redemptive work of Christ effective for our lives and futures, the Holy Spirit becomes God's greatest gift to his people, because in and through him all the fullness of God's gifts are to be found. This is clearly the meaning intended in Luke 11:9–13, where Jesus urges his disciples to trust God's gracious nature as Father by asking him to meet their needs. In the parallel account in Matthew 7:7–11, Jesus' concluding words are, "If you then, who are evil, know how to give good gifts to your children, how much more will your Father in heaven give good things to those who ask him!" In Luke's account, however, "good things" is replaced by "the Holy Spirit." The Spirit is God's ultimate gift. It is through the Spirit that all lesser gifts are conveyed to meet our daily needs.

This ultimacy of the Spirit as gift is made clear in Jesus' encounter with the Samaritan woman in John 4. When Jesus asks her for a drink of water from Jacob's well, she responds with puzzlement, since Jews regarded Samaritan utensils (such as cups) as ritually unclean. Jesus counters with a mysterious and compelling statement: "If you knew the gift of God, and who it is that is saying to you, 'Give me a drink,' you would have asked him, and he would have given you living water" (4:10). This prompts the woman to deeper investigation, and ultimately she receives what her soul thirsts for. "Living water" here is a metaphor for the Holy Spirit (see John 7:37–39, where John identifies the two clearly). The fullness of life that Jesus offers is encapsulated in the gift of the Spirit, the living water that satisfies for eternity. The Spirit is the gift of God that keeps on giving.

One of the primary ways in which this continuous giving of the Spirit is seen is in the outpouring of "spiritual gifts" upon the church. Though in a more general sense God the Father is the author of all these gifts, the Spirit serves as the agent through whom the gifts are given, and the one who sovereignly determines which gifts are given to whom at what points in time. In 1 Corinthians 12:8–10 Paul offers a representative list of spiritual gifts, and concludes: "All these are inspired by one and the same Spirit, who apportions to each one individually as he wills."

The topic of spiritual gifts continues to generate much controversy in the life of the church. Well-intentioned Christians are divided over how to define the various gifts listed in the Scriptures, how to determine what the most important gifts are, what gifts are "available" in this present age, whether the gift of speaking in tongues is necessary for all believers as a sign of their spiritual vitality, whether gifts are a temporary or permanent possession of the believer, and how the more spectacular gifts are to be utilized in the life of the church. Such controversy is not new. In Paul's day the church at Corinth seethed with conflicting passions over the use and misuse of genuine spiritual gifts. The apostle expends a lot of ink in 1 Corinthians 11:17–14:40 dealing with particular abuses and misunderstandings. Further biblical material can be found in Romans 12, Ephesians 4 and 1 Peter 4.

Perhaps we can regain a bit of equilibrium in the modern debate by starting with some simple observations. Many more staid, mainline Christians have fled the field in the past, assuming that spiritual gifts are the province of particular churches often labeled

"Pentecostal" or "charismatic." Pentecostal churches obviously take their name from the Pentecost experience of the church in Acts 2, and typically emphasize the experience of speaking in tongues as a necessary sign of being a Christian, or at least a "Spirit-filled" Christian.[18] Charismatic churches are named after the Greek word for "gifts" (*charismata*), and typically encourage the experience of a wide range of spiritual gifts. While not necessarily focused on the evidence of tongues, they tend to emphasize the "power gifts" (activities that cannot be mistaken for natural human abilities, such as healings, demonic expulsions, words of knowledge, discernment of spirits and interpretation of tongues). As a consequence, the less "spectacular" gifts are often overlooked or underappreciated.

Yet the New Testament portrays the gifts of the Spirit as valuable on the basis of how well they build up the body of Christ to maturity, not on how well they seem to illustrate the supernatural working of God. For Paul, the underlying principle for ranking gifts in order of importance is: "Let all things be done for building up" (1 Cor. 14:26). To be sure, Paul was seeking to counter a movement in the church at Corinth that elevated the spiritual importance of tongues precisely because it was humanly unintelligible and therefore seemingly more supernatural. Edification must mean, in the first instance, the education of the body of Christ as to the nature and purposes of God in our midst. That is why Paul highlights prophecy as the greatest of gifts. Those who prophesy in the Spirit speak God's Word directly to his people and deepen our understanding of how we are to act in light of Christ's leadership. Yet it is fair to say that in different circumstances, other gifts from the Spirit may equally contribute to the edification of the gathered church. For "building up" is not only a matter of the mind, but also of heart and body. Miracles and healings may contribute to the strengthening of faith and health; acts of mercy, giving and "helps" restore a people emotionally; teaching, preaching and exhortation serve not only to increase knowledge but deepen the heart of commitment; administration and service streamline the efficiency and effectiveness with which God's love is manifested to the community and the world. In all these settings, though, the growth of the church remains the key; the level of perceived "spirituality" or "supernatural power" involved in the exercise of the gifts is never the measure of their value.

In the end, *all* of the gifts of the Spirit are valuable, but only as they are practiced in love, that is, with the intention of serving the welfare of others and avoiding self-promotion. It is no accident that Paul's famous "love chapter"—1 Corinthians 13—occurs precisely in the middle of his discussion of spiritual gifts. Our fallen nature easily leads us to the sin of pride in the form of self-aggrandizement when we talk about spiritual gifts. We naturally want the "best" gifts, and often enviously compare our lot with that of others, wishing we had their constellation of gifts. Or, on the other hand, we feel we have been amply blessed with the gifts most sought after in our tradition, unlike the poor souls around us, and we wallow in pompous self-satisfaction.

Two false presuppositions often accompany all this contentiousness. The first is that whatever gifts we have received from the Spirit have been given us because we somehow deserve them. This is rarely affirmed on the conscious level, but dwells in the background of our psyches and urges us to make comparisons so as to determine our relative worth in the body of Christ. Paul has strong warnings about this in 1 Corinthians 12 and Romans 12, where he condemns the arrogance of individualistic posturing and champions instead the view that we are all equally important because we belong to the same body and each performs an equally needed function for the health of the whole body. The second false presupposition rests upon the belief that possession equals ownership. Evidence of this perspective is readily apparent in how Christians talk about spiritual gifts in their lives: "What's *your* gift?" "*My* gift is . . ." (emphasis on the individual in question). Again, often more subconsciously than deliberately, we act as though we own the gifts granted to us rather than recognizing that we are stewards of abilities and resources provided by the Spirit and to be used for his purposes. The ownership model feeds our ego, and typically leads to an attitude of self-assurance, as though I can pull out my gifts at any time and put them to use at my discretion, for my own agenda—much like the credit cards in my wallet. But anyone who has spent much time in ministry in the name of Jesus knows that gifts do not function this way. Often when I feel most "prepared" for ministry, the gifts do not flow in the way I envision; sometimes they do not flow at all. On other occasions when I feel least "spiritual" or strong, God seems to work most powerfully through an unprepared statement, a simple prayer or a small, impulsive act of kindness. In the final analysis, spiritual gifts are not our private possessions, nor do we have the right to "manage" the exercise of them in a self-serving way. Rather, as in all other blessings from God, we are called to be stewards of their use in ways that bring glory to him. As Paul indicates, this means that they are to become a concrete expression of love for others, particularly those in the body of Christ, for the purpose of building up God's people to maturity—to "the stature of the fullness of Christ" (Eph. 4:13). So all the gifts of the Spirit are important, and if the church ignores some and champions others, it is diminished in the process.

That leads us to the next question: Which spiritual gifts are available to the church today? In particular, are the so-called sign gifts (miracles, healings, words of knowledge, tongues and interpretation of tongues) still being granted by the Spirit (as they were for the New Testament church) for the growth of the body of Christ, or did these cease after the time of the apostles? As you might expect, the answers vary depending on the group you ask. Pentecostal and charismatic traditions affirm enthusiastically that the Spirit is just as much in the business of signs and wonders today as he ever was. Across the third world especially, this movement is the fastest growing Christian group, and reports of God's extraordinary activities through ordinary followers of Christ are more often the rule rather than the exception. In essence, the charismatic answer to the question is typically, "Of course the Spirit still provides these gifts—we know because we are experiencing them regularly."

Other groups have argued for theological reasons that these gifts are no longer given. What charismatics claim as valid spiritual gifts are in fact either spurious (produced by human imagination and wish fulfillment) or produced by demonic supernatural powers seeking to deceive God's people. In either case, they say, such "signs and wonders" are counterfeit and thus to be avoided.

In particular, some argue that charismatic gifts are extinct because their original purpose was fulfilled in the time of the apostles.What then was the original purpose of these obsolete "supernatural gifts"? Some say it was to provide divine credentials for the apostles as they undertook their fledgling mission of convincing the world that they spoke for God. But once the apostolic church was firmly established and the authority of Jesus' original witnesses accepted by increasing numbers, the need for authenticating miracles diminished. Hence with the passing of the apostolic age came the cessation of such sign gifts.

Others argue that what needed authenticating was not the apostles themselves but the message of the gospel until it could be gathered into the inspired written form we now know as the New Testament. Special sign gifts were necessary while the Word of God remained in oral form and therefore subject to the distortion of false prophets or rival religious groups. But once the Word of God was gathered authoritatively in written form and recognized by the people of God as inspired by the Holy Spirit, there remained no significant purpose for signs and wonders. Hence they were withdrawn by the Spirit from the field of play once the scriptural canon was closed.

These arguments, however, prove less than satisfactory. First, there is no clear biblical warrant for suggesting that the obviously miraculous gifts are meant *only* for authenticating the first-century message or messenger. It seems clear in Paul's mind that the fundamental purpose of all the gifts (including healings, miracles, supernatural guidance, etc.) is to build up and minister to the body of Christ. What would we be saying about God if we argued that God performed miracles in the first century AD not primarily out of love for human beings in need but rather out of a desire to authenticate his message? Would not human beings become a means to an end, and not an end in themselves? This is certainly not the image that the Gospels leave us with, where Jesus is moved with compassion for the harrassed and helpless, where he intervenes with supernatural ability to release victims from physical, emotional or spiritual captivity. Is it not preferable biblically to argue that God has multiple purposes in blessing the church with spiritual gifts, including *both* the care of his creation and the authentication of the preached gospel? In this case, we would expect the kinds of gifts in question to continue their vital role in the Spirit's ministry throughout the earthly existence of the church.

And this is exactly what we see in the church's history over the last two thousand years. For every century there are significant, substantive reports of God's miraculous activity through the instrumentality of believers exercising their ministries. Equally important, in the church's contemporary experience around the world reports abound concerning the reality of "sign gifts." Missionaries raised and trained in the rationalistic, Enlightenment age of the West and sent off to the third world come back on furlough years later full of stories about how God is powerfully at work among his people.

But perhaps most compelling is that Jesus seemed to make clear that all the gifts of the Spirit are part of the new age of the kingdom of God. He exercised these gifts himself, then authorized and commanded his disciples to proclaim the inbreaking of the kingdom in both word and deed. In John 14:12 Jesus declares to the fledgling church, "Very truly, I tell you, the one who believes in me will also do the works that I do and, in fact, will do greater works than these, because I am going to the Father." The Gospel writer Luke picks up on this theme in creating the second of his New Testament works, the book of Acts. In its introduction he refers back to his Gospel as containing that which Jesus *began* to do and teach, making clear by inference that he intended Acts to be an account of what Jesus, after his ascension, continued to do and teach through the young church. The ministry gifts granted believers by the Spirit are simply a continuation of what Jesus set in motion through his earthly ministry. Paul's metaphor of the church as the body of Christ further underscores this New Testament teaching that the community of Jesus' followers is to incarnate the same ministry that Jesus concerned himself with during his earthly life. Since Jesus' activities involved both word and works, so will those of his disciples.

If, then, we can expect that the Spirit still graces the church with the full range of gifts at his disposal, the obvious question that arises is, Why don't we typically see these power gifts in the mainline churches?

The answer is to be found at least partly in the fact that the mainline churches have been most heavily influenced by an Enlightenment worldview that eliminates the supernatural and nonrational from the realms of possibility, or at least from practical likelihood. Our ministers and our membership have been trained in an educational system saddled with a secular worldview, and bring this bias into their ministries. After generations of such an approach, modern-day churches have little positive inclination to expect the miraculous. The existing models of those that do are not very attractive to folks raised in the mainline church environment.

This predisposition not to believe in the present existence of sign gifts can then become a self-fulfilling prophecy. Remember Jesus' return to his hometown of Nazareth, and the skepticism that greeted his ministry there? Jesus chastised them with the statement, "A prophet is not without honor except in his own country," and Matthew comments upon this event that "he did not do many deeds of power there, because of their unbelief" (Matt. 13:54–58). Where there is no expectation, there will be no faith. Where there is no faith, God generally eschews the demonstration of his glory with power.

If, then, the sign gifts are being offered by the Spirit today for the well-being of the body of Christ and for extended service to the world, what steps ought Reformed congregations take to utilize these gifts?

First, we must deal with our lack of expectation by realizing that we are children of our secularized age, which has sold us a bill of goods concerning God. Rather than taking our cue from the clear witness of Scripture in both Old and New Testaments, we have quietly written off the immediate communication and miraculous activity of God from our lives. Yet if God is indeed the same yesterday, today and forever (see Heb. 13:8), then it is logical to conclude that the same Spirit who moved with power through Moses, Elijah and Paul, and who spoke authoritatively through Samuel,

Nathan and Priscilla, remains at work today in the midst of his people. As post-Pentecost people who live fully in the age of the Spirit, we must retrain ourselves to come with openness to worship gatherings, expecting that through the gifts of others God will bring blessing to us, and through us God will minister powerfully to the needs of those around us.

Second, in yielding ourselves to the sovereignty of the Spirit, we must not demand or disallow any gifts he should wish to grant us. Our calling is to be willing instruments for service, however God should choose to use us. Since we know that God's will generally is for the growth and maturity of the church, our desire should mirror the Spirit's intent in granting gifts to his people. In this sense, we are to "earnestly desire the greater gifts," and to be open to the Spirit's leading in how we may minister most beneficially for the larger body of Christ. With regard to the sign gifts, this means that we are neither to seek to force the Spirit's hand by demanding or assuming that certain gifts (tongues, healings, etc.) accompany the experience of being filled with the Spirit for ministry, nor to avoid the Spirit's grace by ignoring or categorically rejecting gifts foreign to our limited experience. With increasing maturity comes the realization that while the experience of supernatural power can be thrilling, God exercises his might not to thrill spectators but to glorify himself through the defeat of evil and the restoration of the creation.

Third, we must keep before us the truth that while the Spirit operates in sovereign freedom, he does not create confusion. Not only worship but also ministry "in the Spirit" should be characterized by order and purpose. Nowhere does the biblical witness model what goes on in some congregations: increasingly frenzied incantations against evil spirits, the mindless repetition of meaningless syllables, those in ministry jumping around the sanctuary and bellowing commands in the name of God. Indeed, the Spirit is full of surprises, and those under his guidance may be called to great risks of faith, but these types of behaviors smack more of the fallen human spirit's attempt to muster up some attention for itself rather than of the divine Spirit's sovereign work in advancing the kingdom of God. Paul makes clear that the expression of even the more ecstatic gifts remains under the control of the individual in question, so that gatherings of worship and ministry should never be characterized by disorder, frenzy or mindlessness (see 1 Cor. 14:26–40). They are to be used for the glory of God.

Fourth, whatever gifts the Spirit grants us, we are to exercise them in love. That is, our agenda is to be the increased welfare of those in need around us, regardless of the cost to ourselves in time, energy or even stature among the worldly. Servant-hearted love demands humility, and those who wish to follow in the ministry footsteps of the Lord Jesus must be careless of their reputation, willing to risk new ventures as the Spirit deepens our effectiveness.

One final word about the categorization of spiritual gifts. A natural human tendency is to want to establish once and for all the complete list of gifts provided by the Spirit to the church, together with a detailed definition of what they entail and how they function. However, a quick look at the New Testament passages dealing with gifts (see above) should make us cautious in this regard. Although Paul offers lists in Romans 12:6–8, 1 Corinthians 12:8–10 and Ephesians 4:11, they all show significant variety. Sometimes he focuses on gifts as concrete actions (e.g., evangelism, prophecy, healings, acts of mercy); other times he envisages gifts in terms of the long-term ministries granted individuals within the body of Christ (e.g., evangelist, prophet, healer, pastor). This variety of substance and approach as well as our understanding of the Spirit's sovereign nature should make us wary of defining too precisely the boundaries of spiritual gifting. It is not our place to decide what the Spirit can or cannot do to empower Christ's followers for ministry, nor would we be wise to classify and delimit gifts so precisely that we neglect the Spirit's leading in new or unanticipated situations.

Perhaps a better approach than the exhaustive list is the analogy of the body. Using Paul's favorite image of the church as the living body of Christ, and of the Spirit as the animating force of that body, we may say that spiritual gifts are the ministering abilities of the living body. For convenience' sake, they may be grouped according to function, but always with the realization that the full range of the body's function resists simple categorization. Thus we have *gifts of discernment* (the eyes of the body) such as supernatural wisdom and knowledge and discerning of spirits, that, when applied to specific situations, lead God's people to act in ways they would not have discovered by mere reason and experience alone. We are strengthened as well by *gifts of speech* (the mouth of the body) such as prophecy, teaching, preaching, exhortation, tongues and interpretation of tongues, by which the church is instructed, comforted, challenged, commanded and edified. Third, there are what we might call *gifts of power and compassion* (the hands of the body), such as healings, miracles, giving, helps and mercy. These are the vehicles through which the mercy and kindness of God are robustly displayed in meeting the bodily, material and emotional needs of those seeking Christ's help.

All of these gifts are part of the arsenal of the Spirit against the destructive powers of the kingdom of this age. Though no individual exhibits all of them, they are fully available to us through the healthy functioning of the entire body of Christ. Thus we are caught up together in the dance of the Spirit, who uses us in Christ's name to serve others, and our brothers and sisters in Christ to serve us through the multivarious manifestations of spiritual gifts. These intended blessings can become divisive when wielded by immature believers who are more concerned with their own self-perceived spiritual potency than they are with serving others, but in the lives of mature disciples the gifts function as the concrete expressions of the love of God for his children and for the world at large. They reflect the irrepressible character of God's Holy Spirit, who is the gift that keeps on giving.

7

Fruitful Lives

*T*im and I met for lunch at a trendy GenX restaurant. He was home on break from a highly respected university, where among other things he served as a leader for an on-campus Christian organization. He wanted to know from me what Presbyterians believe about the Holy Spirit and one's call to ministry. As his story unfolded, it became clear that God had been at work in his life powerfully, and Tim was wondering whether God might be calling him to some world-changing ministry. "I'm kind of hoping God will give me the gift of being an apostle," he said, "and use me to bring a lot of people into the kingdom."

I sensed in Tim a real yearning to serve Christ, as well as an ambition to stand out in his efforts for God. So we talked about spiritual gifts for a while, about what it means to have a servant's heart and about the dangers of seeking to wield Jesus' power without being clothed in his character. "I'm convinced," I told him, "that God is much more concerned with the kind of people we become than with the things we accomplish on his behalf." Transformation of character is a higher priority than exercise of gifts, because without maturity spiritual gifts can be abused and lead to harm. As part of a mature life, on the other hand, they can be utilized to their full potential.

It is true that growth in maturity as well as in giftedness are both processes, and it would be wrong to wait on serving Christ in any way until we had attained some arbitrary level of maturity. We must, however, be wary of putting young, immature believers in ministry positions of significant authority—much better to let them develop their gifts in smaller settings and at a pace that parallels their overall growth in Christ.

Since deepening Christian maturity is meant to be a high priority for all believers, and since the Holy Spirit occupies the central place in the development of this maturity in Christ, we would be wise to take time to consider in some detail how God's Spirit deepens our humanity, reshaping us from our misshapen fallen natures into a new humanity in Christ.

Paul makes clear that God's intention for us has always been to salvage our human nature and make it perfect—like that of his incarnate Son. So we are told in Romans 8:29–30 that God sovereignly oversees the process of our transformation from beginning to end, from our initial election in Christ to our ultimate glorification ("For those whom he foreknew he also predestined to be conformed to the image of his Son.... And those whom he predestined he also called; and those whom he called he also justified; and those whom he justified he also glorified"[19]). And Paul assumes as a primary task[20] the nurturing of believers along this path of growth into Christlikeness, for since Christ in us is our only hope of glory, the proclamation of the gospel and ongoing exhortation and teaching of Christians is essential "so that we may present everyone mature in Christ" (Col. 1:28).

What does this mature life, produced by the Spirit and tended by divinely called teachers and preachers, look like? Much of the New Testament is taken up with this question, from the Gospel accounts of Jesus' human life (which we are called to emulate) to the apostles' letters to various churches (which deal with specific questions of how believers are to live in the midst of an alien [ungodly] culture). But perhaps the best shorthand description of the mature Christian life is found in Paul's discussion of the fruit of the Spirit (Gal. 5:22–25), where he places the activities and orientation of new life in Christ over against that of our old, natural life in the flesh:

> By contrast, the fruit of the Spirit is love, joy, peace, patience, kindness, generosity, faithfulness, gentleness and self-control.

There is no law against such things. And those who belong to Christ have crucified the flesh with its passions and desires. If we live by the Spirit, let us also be guided by the Spirit.

The agricultural image of fruit bearing makes clear that the nine qualities listed by Paul were not seen by him as add-ons to normal life, things that we must put on our to-do lists for the day and try to accomplish before falling exhausted into bed each night. Rather they are the natural outworking of the new life of Christ within us. The idea is that as we regularly nurture our life-giving connection with Jesus, the true source of these virtues, they naturally begin to develop as fruit among the branches of our daily lives. Paul was not the first to express this truth in agricultural terms. In the Gospel of John (15:1–8) Jesus speaks of himself as the true vine of Israel (the one who bears fruit that really pleases his Father). If he is the vine (that is, the root stock from which all the branches of the grapevine grow), then his disciples are seen as the branches through whom the fruit of love is actually produced. It is possible to be a branch that produces no fruit, but such branches, says Jesus, are cut off and destroyed. Their problem is that they were never really anchored in the vine stock, the trunk through which the life-giving, fruit-producing resources run liberally. Jesus warns his followers, "Apart from me you can do nothing" (15:5), but encourages them with the flip side of the coin, "Those who abide in me and I in them bear much fruit." The message is clear: the fruit of spiritual maturity comes not by autonomous, moral effort, but by the infusion of a new kind of life available only to those who discipline themselves to stay close to the Lord in everyday life.

We must be clear about this. The New Testament knows nothing of a "pull yourself up by the bootstraps" morality. The Christian life is not about a reformation of morals; it is about the destruction of an old kind of life and the birth of a new kind, the uprooting of a bad tree and replanting it with a good tree. Moral reform might entail stripping the bad tree of its malodorous fruit and taping onto it artificial fruit that looks very appetizing—a lot of effort to produce something pleasing to the eyes but yielding no change in the basic nature of the tree. Left to itself, it will still produce malodorous fruit. If you want good fruit from that plot of land, you must cut down and root out the old tree, and plant a new tree, whose nature it is to produce good fruit.

So Paul says in Galatians 5:19–21 that the life of the flesh (our natural, untreated state) produces unholy fruit: "fornication, impurity, licentiousness, idolatry, sorcery, enmities, strife, jealousy, anger, quarrels, dissensions, factions, envy, drunkenness, carousing, and things like these." It is clear that this is not an exhaustive list, but one meant to frame the kinds of behaviors and attitudes naturally cultivated by the fallen human heart. Our unredeemed nature produces only this kind of fruit. No matter how hard we try to reform them, our sinful proclivities remain focused on a "me-first, get out of my way" approach to life. They will never desire the goals that a life directed by the Spirit of God embraces—"For what the flesh desires is opposed to the Spirit, and what the Spirit desires is opposed to the flesh" (Gal. 5:17).

The lifestyle qualities sketched in verses 22–23 represent generally what the Spirit desires to produce in us, although Paul makes clear that as his list of the works of the flesh is not exhaustive neither is this catalog of nine virtues. In verse 23 he declares that "there is no law against *such things*," indicating that all other human virtues that we might name also find their ultimate source in the work of the Spirit.

Interestingly, when Paul speaks of the outgrowth of fallen human efforts, he employs the plural "*works* of the flesh," but when he turns to the harvest of the truly spiritual life he employs the singular "*fruit* of the Spirit." Perhaps in the first instance his purpose is to reflect a sense of disharmony or chaos associated with the whims of human passion. In the second instance we are called to see the unity and harmony involved in what the Spirit creates in our lives. The fruit of the Spirit is like a bunch of grapes, singular in the sense that it is all "the fruit of the vine," but plural in the sense that each grape in the bunch is an element distinct from all the others. They are all produced together as part of the whole bunch, and are meant to be integrally related in the life of the believer. We do not look over the list of spiritual fruit in this section and highlight which individual elements we want to have in our lives (or which we would rather not be bothered with). Rather, we discover that the Spirit's intent is to produce all of these (and more) in our lives, which he will do as we yield ourselves to his control, or, in Paul's words, as we walk in the Spirit.

It is important to recognize that when we come to faith in Christ as Savior and Lord, we hand ourselves over unconditionally to God. We enroll ourselves in his spiritual health clinic for the full treatment. If God's purpose is indeed to reproduce in us the perfect life of his Son, then he will not stop until the old life has been finally destroyed and the new life fully developed, a life now characterized by the full and permanent display of all the fruit of the Spirit.

Therefore, unlike the gifts of the Spirit, which are portioned out to all believers in such a way that no individual ministers with all the gifts but operates interdependently with the rest of the body of Christ in sharing the gifts for the mutual benefit of the church, the fruit of the Spirit is a new reality that God intends each believer in Christ to experience ultimately in its completeness. Right now we are on the road to this fullness of life, or, to stay with our agricultural metaphor, we are young grapevine saplings of various sizes and shapes, all of whom are producing some fruit, but nowhere near the amount and quality we will produce when we have reached complete maturity and the vinedresser has had his way with us. This process of growth Reformed theologians have always called "sanctification." It is a process of transformation that begins when we first enter into the life of apprenticeship to Jesus Christ and that continues through our remaining earthly life. During this time, the Spirit increasingly weans us from our old manner of life and develops in us the virtues of heaven. A sure-fire method for determining our growth over time is to assess (often through the eyes of those who know us best) what kind of progress we are making in becoming more loving, joyful, peaceful, patient and so on. If the Spirit is indeed in us, and we are seeking to walk in his power, then we will see such fruit in increasing measure. What is true of believers as individuals will also be true of the local church, the gathered body of believers. We ought to be able to apply the same test to assess the maturity level of our congregations. Hence the best measure of spiritual depth in a church is not its level of biblical knowledge or financial giving, or its record in membership growth, worship attendance or community ministries. These may serve as pointers to spiritual life, but in themselves they prove nothing definitive. But strong evidence of the fruit of the Spirit among the church community members is an undeniable evidence of the long-term working of the Holy Spirit, for such spiritual fruit cannot be counterfeited in a group setting any more than it can be feigned in the life of an individual.

If we understand this, and wish these realities to become the regular patterns of our lives, then two obvious questions follow: How does the Spirit produce such fruit in us? and What role do we play in bearing the fruit of the Spirit? Though these are often thought to be esoteric questions, we will spend the remainder of this chapter seeking to provide down-to-earth answers that help us in practical ways to grow in Christ.

How does the Holy Spirit produce fruit in human lives? Is this an impersonal, automatic process? Can we expect that anyone who belongs to a church and claims an association with Christ will evidence this deep spiritual transformation? Clearly the answer to the last two questions must be no. The God who reveals himself to human beings as the epitome of love never does anything in an impersonal way, never acts mechanistically toward the creatures he has loved into existence. So the first thing we can say, and perhaps the only thing we can say with full confidence, is that spiritual fruit develops in the context of a living relationship with God in the person of the Holy Spirit. Not only does the Spirit bring us to new life in Christ, but as he continues to dwell within us and interact with our lives, he produces the fruit of transformed hearts, minds and wills.

Beyond this it is difficult to say much with certainty about the mysterious workings of the Spirit. After all, as the major biblical images of the Spirit make clear, his efforts, like the wind, are typically invisible to the physical eye; like breath, he is difficult to separate from the inmost parts of our being; like water, he seeps into deep crevasses of our souls and inscrutably penetrates what formerly seemed impervious to change, much as water makes wet whatever comes into contact with it; like fire, he is both unpredictable and wild, yet at the same time brings the warmth needed for life to flourish.

Perhaps it is helpful to think of the Spirit's impact on human lives as analogous to a "good infection." People show the symptoms of the flu not simply when they have been exposed to the flu virus, but when their bodies have shown hospitality to the virus and enabled it to gain a foothold and begin its replication process within their biological systems. In other words, to use our everyday language about such sicknesses, the flu must be "caught." Once that has happened, the virus quite naturally goes about its work of producing the various symptoms of headaches, fever, chills, nausea and the consequent desire to crawl off somewhere and die. People are not "taught" how to have the flu—they just catch it (though some children seek to perfect the art of imitating the illness during certain weeks at school). In a parallel way, though with happier results, the Spirit of God must also be "caught"; life in the Spirit cannot be "taught," though some people, never exposed to the real thing, seek to imitate the life they see others living. For those "infected" with the Spirit, their actions and attitudes begin to show the symptoms of his presence. These are what Paul refers to as the fruit of the Spirit. They are the natural outflow of the work of the Holy Spirit in the lives of those in whom he takes up residence.

This should not surprise us. The Holy Spirit has been charged with the task of continuing the ministry that Jesus inaugurated when he announced the invasion of the kingdom of God into this fallen world. Jesus began the "good infection" by rubbing elbows with those needing an infusion of health. When the sick came to him, even those like lepers whose presence threatened to spread the contagion of illness and evil, Jesus reached out and healed them with his touch and word. Instead of the powerful contagion of sickness and sin spreading from others to him, the much more powerful contagion of grace and healing spread from Jesus to them. So it continues today for us, for all those whose path the Holy Spirit crosses.

Though this analogy of the Spirit to a "good virus" is helpful, we need to address a few potential misconceptions lest we drift unwittingly into unbiblical, non-Reformed thinking about the Spirit's relationship to us. Unlike with a virus, we do not "catch" the Spirit by accident or chance. True, there are things we can do to put ourselves in the best position to experience the presence of the Spirit, and we will address these matters below, but they are secondary. Since the Spirit is God, he remains sovereign and purposive. We do not "catch" the Spirit as much as we respond to his loving initiative. He comes to us with conscious purpose and intent, seeking to make a new home in our lives. We can and do resist his advances because of our naturally sinful natures, but he is able to overcome our recalcitrance and turn our wills toward himself. When this happens, and we subsequently welcome his presence, the Spirit takes up residence in us. To use Jesus' words of John 14:17 regarding his disciples' receiving the Spirit willingly, "You know him, for he dwells with you, and will be in you."

Unlike with a virus, then, the Spirit's nearness to us is not due to chance or accident, but due to the relentless love of God that refuses to leave us to our own increasing hellishness. By sovereign, divine power, he awakens us to new life and woos and coaxes us to respond as a mother coos to her newborn and strokes its cheeks and offers her breast to initiate a life-giving relationship that will grow and mature over the years.

Also unlike a virus, the effect of the Spirit in us is not to destroy but to enhance our well-being. We typically see "contagion" and "infection" as negatives, for they are almost always used in connection with disease or social blight. But the impact of the Spirit is well described as a contagion of new life invading and supplanting the sin-diseased old life that has run rampant through our bodies and souls from the moment we sucked our first breaths of air. So the battle that rages in the lives of all Christians is a battle of new life against old, of life in Christ versus life in the flesh, of the power of the Spirit over against the power of sin within us. The fact that there is a battle is a good sign—it means that we are no longer dead spiritually and thereby oblivious to the call to a new existence. Were we still immersed in an unchallenged life of sin, our consciences would be at peace and we would feel relatively content with our worldly lifestyles. It is the enlivening work of the Spirit in our hearts that first brings us to awareness that we are not living as we ought. He quickens our conscience and grants us new desires that clash with our old habits and obsessions. Because of the Spirit's gift of new life, we find within ourselves a war brewing between the way of Christ and the way of self. As this new life grows and is nurtured, it begins to choke out our old nature. But as we know only too well, the old life does not want to be supplanted, and it fights tooth and nail to keep control of our thoughts and actions, or at least to be left alone in the privacy of our inner world. But as Jesus made clear in the Sermon on the Mount (Matthew 5–7), God's goal for human life is nothing less than our becoming perfect (5:48), thoroughly righteous in thought, word and deed. So the Spirit's program of renovation demands nothing less than the ultimate eradication of sin and evil from our natures. This present life serves as the battleground where he weans us from our desires for evil and establishes in us new tastes and hungers. He spreads the contagion of holiness in and through us, even as our defeated sinful nature seeks to oppose it. In the end, evil will lose. As an old Asian saying has it, "The perfume of holiness travels even against the wind." But for now, the battle rages on.

One last contrast. The goal of a virus in spreading itself to other hosts is self-preservation. Put simply, viruses are parasites. They feed off other living things and spread by using their hosts' resources to replicate themselves so as to maintain their presence in this universe. If a virus has its way, it will continue to feed off its host until its replicated presence overwhelms the host and causes death. The virus's "intention" is not to kill its host, but its prime directive is to spread its own existence, which can only be done at the cost of its host. The way of the Holy Spirit is completely contrary to this. When the Spirit invades our bodies and souls, he comes to bring healing and fullness, to give of his endless resources for our benefit, not to take from us. He does not feed off us, but allows us to feed off him. Far from being a parasite, he offers himself and heaven's boundless resources as our host. As we embrace this new dependency on him for the life God calls us to live, and receive the outpouring of vitality impossible to manufacture for ourselves, we grow in the grace, knowledge and love of Jesus Christ.

In 1985 Zimbabwe was in the midst of a five-year drought. Ilene Bradberry told of her experience coping with scant resources in the arid African surroundings:

> I was in the garden trying to keep the few remaining plants alive by pouring leftover dishwater on them—when it began to rain. Now, for days, we had been hiring a boy to ladle buckets of water on our small plot just to keep the shriveled plants alive. It took him all day just to carry enough buckets to sprinkle the half-acre plot. But in five minutes of heavy rain, the whole garden was soaked, the entire yard, all of the neighbors' yards and in fact the entire city. If we were to calculate how much water and how many hours of human effort would have been needed to achieve the same ends, it would have been mind-boggling and humanly overwhelming. God did it all in five minutes of heavy rainfall, with no effort on our part.
>
> I stood in the rain letting it soak into my dry skin and parched garden, realizing how many times I've wanted to take matters into my own hands and manipulate circumstances through lots of human effort, when God was waiting for me to let him do it his way much more effectively.

A simple truth, and yet so often we find ourselves filling up buckets to water the deserts of our hearts. In the end, no matter how hard we try, the dryness is too great, our strength too small, the water in too short supply. The gospel makes clear that only God can adequately quench our spiritual thirst. Only he deals in living water, which causes human souls to grow and flourish.

It is clear, then, that the Spirit of God plays the determinative role in our becoming more like Jesus. Does that mean that we are always passive, merely being acted upon by divine sovereignty, being re-created in the image of Christ no matter what we do, or fail to do? Obviously, this cannot be the case. Any relationship worth its salt requires the meaningful interaction of both parties. Where love is involved, that interaction may often best be characterized in terms of dance, the choreography of give and take, of initiative and response, embracing and being embraced. So it is with the Holy Spirit and the believer in Christ. As we have seen already, the Spirit is the Trinity's initiative of love stirring us to life through the electing call of God in Jesus Christ. It is he who awakens us spiritually, who draws us upward and inward to the center of life, who empowers us and grants all the tools needed for maturing into the perfect beings God envisions us becoming. But this does not happen automatically.

The Scriptures make clear time and again that God calls us to respond to his overtures of love, to exercise our wills to walk by faith, to act in the world on the basis of our trust in the divine promises found in the Bible, to open ourselves to the life of Christ so that every day, every hour, every moment, we think, intend, dream, hope, speak, act, surrender to the Father, with the mind of Christ. What would it be like for us to live in unbroken dependence on God, in full communion with him so that every thought, word and deed of ours was inhabited by God, so that God permeated the world through us and graced his creation through us with love and justice, with healing and wisdom, with peace and joy? Perhaps that is too much for us to imagine, knowing our fallen hearts as well as we do. Nevertheless, God's redemptive intention in the life of every Christian, indeed his goal for the church, is to present us before himself "in splendor, without spot or wrinkle or any such thing, that she [the church] might be holy and without blemish" (Eph. 5:27). The Holy Spirit pours into us his life for this very purpose, but we must make use of this life, by tending to the inner flames in the hearth of our soul, by stoking the fire born of the Spirit with the fuel of his grace.

> For this very reason [i.e., that we may become partakers of the divine nature through God's precious and very great promises], you must make every effort to support your faith with goodness, and goodness with knowledge, and knowledge with self-control, and self-control with endurance, and endurance with godliness, and godliness with mutual affection, and mutual affection with love. For if these things are yours and are increasing among you, they keep you from being ineffective and unfruitful in the knowledge of our Lord Jesus Christ. (2 Pet. 1:5–8)

The Bible is filled with stories of how God's followers struggled to keep the inner fires burning, some with great success, others with regrettable failure. But woven throughout the story of God's people are the threads of experience that show us clearly a variety of means of grace whereby we can remain alive and vital in the Spirit, increasingly partaking of the divine nature. These means of grace have become known in the church as *spiritual disciplines.* For those committed to the pursuit of spiritually fruitful lives, they are indispensable, as we will see in the coming chapter.

8

Furrows in the Heart

*G*rowing up in the arid eastern province of Saudi Arabia, I saw my fill of parched, lifeless land. It was not that the ground refused to grow anything. When winter rains came, parts of the desert would erupt with colorful vegetation at the edges of gathered pools left in wadis and basins. But when the rains ceased, and the floods had fully dried up, the desert blooms would soon follow suit. There were a few exceptions to this pattern, however.

About ten miles from where we lived, across sand dunes and salt flats, was the sparkling oasis of al-Hofuf. While one could make the drive on fifteen miles of regular roads, I knew the desert path, because as Boy Scouts we used to trek to the oasis and back as part of earning a hiking merit badge. An oasis is a wonderful sight after trudging over sand hills and across crusty ground where the only signs of life are scrub brush, sidewinders, lizards, the odd scorpion or two and ubiquitous flies. The memories of feeling hot, thirsty, dusty and tired, cresting a final dune to see the green jewel of Hofuf, racing the other Scouts to reach the underground, spring-fed pools, stripping down to our shorts and diving into the relief of the deep, clear blue waters of the oasis, still causes my skin to tingle with delight. But deep blue is not the only color impressed on my memory. Impossible to forget are the rich greens as well. Floral life stretches for long distances from the oasis. Why? Because the Saudis have dug an intricate latticework of furrows from the springs to the fertile land around the life-giving waters. These irrigation trenches allow water to be channeled regularly to otherwise arid ground so they can produce an abundance of crops.

The Saudis have learned well what all farmers in harsh, dry environments know: when precious water is available, it must be used to the fullest extent possible, if sufficient crops are to be produced. The digging of irrigation ditches, the building of canals and aqueducts to carry runoff or spring water from saturated areas to dry ones, the plowing and tilling of hard earth to enable water to soak deeper, all of these are disciplines used by societies where rains and rivers are sparse and irreplaceable resources.

In just the same way, spiritual disciplines are the activities Christians engage in to prepare the ground of their lives for the living water of the Holy Spirit (one of Jesus' favorite metaphors for the third member of the Trinity—see John 4:10–14; 7:37–39). They are the tools with which we dig furrows in the heart. The deeper and vaster the array, the more we benefit from God's outpoured presence, and the greater our utilization of his power, love and wisdom for everyday spiritual growth.

There is not one divinely authorized, inerrant list of spiritual disciplines. Most catalogs of these Christian disciplines vary depending on traditions and tastes. There is nevertheless a core group of spiritual practices that all Christians agree to be essential in preparing us to receive more fully the transforming grace of God. They are helpful precisely because they facilitate our increased openness to the Spirit of God, by whom alone all true spiritual growth develops.

This point cannot be stressed too much. Spiritual disciplines do not in and of themselves create spiritual growth—they merely expose us more fully to the transforming life of God the Spirit. If approached as a "do-it-yourself" course of improvement, such exercises become a futile effort toward Christlikeness. As Paul makes clear in Colossians 2:23, "These have indeed an appearance of wisdom in promoting self-imposed piety, humility, and severe treatment of the body, but they are of no value in checking self-indulgence." Oftentimes, our increased discipline outwardly appears spiritual to others, but inwardly feeds our pride and arrogance, and so becomes counterproductive to the Christian life. Our own disciplined activities, then, do not make us more mature. But when practiced with the right attitudes, they become channels of the life-giving Spirit, who by his transforming presence does make us more mature.

Spiritual disciplines may be divided generally into two major categories according to their intended focus. Advancement in the life of the kingdom of God involves consistent endeavors on two fronts, the battle against our fallen nature (what the Puritans called "mortification of the flesh") and the nurture of our fledgling life in Christ. Spiritual disciplines focus predominantly in one of these two areas, though a few, as we will see, incorporate both approaches. If they mainly target our inherent, sinful tendencies, they are known as *disciplines of abstinence* and help us break the power of habitual behavior patterns that keep us from pursuing God. If, on the other hand, they seek directly to encourage our love for God and neighbor (the two great commandments upon which the remainder of God's law rests), they are known as *disciplines of engagement.*

As will quickly be seen from the illustrative list below, disciplines of abstinence have a privative function; that is, their aim is to wean us from evil or unhelpful desires, in accordance with biblical teaching: "abstain from the desires of the flesh that wage war against the soul" (1 Pet. 2:11).

> *Disciplines of Abstinence*
> fasting
> simplicity
> silence
> solitude
> chastity
> Sabbath keeping

Being trained in the school of the Spirit to prevail over our out-of-control lusts, we are set free from former masters of personal and interpersonal destruction, and enabled to set our newly unshackled hearts on the pursuit of God. The exercise[21] of these disciplines fulfills in a very practical way Jesus' comment to aspiring disciples, "If any want to become my followers, let them deny themselves and take up their cross daily and follow me" (Luke 9:23).

Fasting, then, becomes a spiritual discipline when it is undertaken not for reasons of vanity (to lose weight) or for medical purposes (e.g., to cleanse the physical body of impurities), but to enable us to grasp more consciously that we do not "live by bread alone, but by every word that comes from the mouth of God" (Matt. 4:4). Our hunger pangs can serve as a regular reminder to turn our thoughts toward God, who is the ultimate satisfaction of our deepest human needs. In this way, fasting clears the decks of our lives for a while, and drives home to our bodies and minds that there is an even more basic requirement for our lives than food.

Simplicity is the discipline of relieving our lives of material clutter. Years ago in Hollywood, Samuel Goldwyn's secretary was trying to free up room in her filing cabinets, so she asked her boss for permission to destroy files that had been inactive for more than ten years. "Go ahead," said the movie baron, "but make sure you keep copies." Many of us have likewise discovered to our dismay that the more we possess, the more we tend to be possessed. The more security we find in things, the less willing we become to part with anything. The fear of losing what we have, or of being without something we "foolishly" let slip through our grasp, works its bedevilment in our lives by convincing us to hang on tightly to what we have, and to back it up with more, lest we be caught unprepared, or lack what society tells us is necessary for a contented life. So we continue to accumulate, and our growing attachments then demand increasing attention lest they deteriorate or get stolen. But the more we set our minds on "earthly things," Jesus reminds us, the less attention we will have for spiritual things (Matt. 6:19–21). The move toward simplicity, on the other hand, throttles the impulse to accumulate as we discipline ourselves to rein in our lifestyles, to give away our excess, to free our time and resources from serving mammon and her daughters to serving the kingdom of God instead.

The discipline of silence trains us to wean ourselves from the cacaphonies of sound both interior and exterior. How much we are addicted to noise is seen in our inability to be content without the radio or television on. Many of us are afraid of silence—afraid of being left only with ourselves, or even worse, with the inescapable presence of God, who is frighteningly unpredictable. Much better, we think, to anesthetize ourselves with music, talk radio or even the bustle of human activity around us so that we may avoid the weight of silence. Our fear of silence is a sign that something is awry within us. Nothing is solved by hiding, however. The discipline of silence weans us from the cloak of sound we use to avoid knowing ourselves and God, and frees us to listen and consequently hear clearly the "still, small voice" of the Spirit without the usual competing sounds of our daily world.

Solitude is a sister discipline to that of silence, though not identical. While silence fasts temporarily from sound, solitude fasts temporarily from society. Just as we can lose ourselves in noise, we can hide from the deeper purpose of life by surrounding ourselves so unremittingly with relationships that they keep us from truly getting to knowing ourselves. The discipline of solitude reminds us that there is more to life than external relationships. While it remains true that we were created for human as well as divine relationship, we can use horizontal relationships as a means of distancing ourselves from God or our own soul. Solitude draws our attention back from the escape of looking only outward. It frees us from the tyranny of defining ourselves through the impressions of others, as well as slavery to our powerful, untamed self. Enough time spent alone in probing examination of our actions and motives leads us to learn more of our inner makeup, our strengths and weaknesses, our tendencies and drives. Such knowledge is the first step to breaking free from slavery to the deep, hidden passions that often drive our behavior and leave us bewildered in the process. It also prepares us for the positive disciplines of confession, prayer and meditation.

Chastity is perhaps the most unpopular discipline of abstinence in our time. It has been increasingly ignored within the life of the Western church as Christians young and old see few if any barriers to cohabitation outside marriage. Sensual pleasure is one of the watchwords of our day, and the more enculturated the church has become, the more we have embraced worldly values. "Free sex," one of the rallying cries of the 1960s, has shown itself to be not without heavy costs, and yet the counsel of sexual chastity outside marriage is received with incredulous laughter or outright scorn for what is taken to be outmoded morality. The virtue and discipline of chastity is desperately needed among Christians. We need to be reminded that sexual pleasure is not the be-all and end-all of life. Certainly it is a blessing created by God for human beings to enjoy, but as with every blessing it is meant to direct our hearts in gratitude more to the Giver rather than the gift. The discipline of chastity develops within us this perspective. We also need to be reminded according to biblical morality that the sexual relationship belongs within the loving commitment of marriage. Outside such a relationship, sexual expression often becomes destructive spiritually as well as socially. The practice of chastity undergirds our adherence to biblical morality and enables us to walk within the safe boundaries of sexual health provided by a gracious God. Finally, we as God's people are called to provide a witness to the larger world of healthy living. This includes how we handle the sexual impulses common to humanity, and winsomely present God's will to a culture that rebels against any restrictions on the pursuit of pleasure. If the church does not model in action the practice of sexual chastity outside marriage, where will the world be challenged to pursue an agenda greater than physical hedonism? The discipline of chastity, then, serves a countercultural, prophetic role in these postmodern, post-Christian days.

Sabbath keeping serves as both a discipline of abstinence and of engagement—it is a bridging practice of spirituality. Regarding abstinence, Sabbath keeping in its simplest form is giving up work so as to rest ("Six days you shall labor and do all your work. But the seventh day is a sabbath to the LORD your God; you shall not do any work—you, your son or your daughter, your male or female slave, your livestock, or the alien resident in your towns" [Exod. 20:9–10]). The Sabbath command reflects the wholesome rhythm of time built into creation ("So God blessed the seventh day and hallowed it, because on it God rested from all the work that he had done in creation" [Gen. 2:3]), and intends that we be set free from the fallen tendency to locate our worth in our accomplishments, and so find ourselves driven to workaholism. This prepares us as well to receive the love of God made known in the grace of Jesus Christ, who embraces us not because we have merited his attention but because he is love incarnate. We are free to work and to rest, secure in God's unchanging and unchangeable grace, which depends not on our accomplishments but on his nature.

> *Disciplines of Engagement*
> Sabbath keeping
> worship
> prayer
> study
> meditation
> confession
> fellowship
> service

But Sabbath keeping is also a spiritual discipline of engagement, because it trains us to do more than simply abstain from the work we do on the other six days of the week. At its best, the Sabbath is meant to be a day of recreation, or re-creation, in God. We are freed from everyday responsibilities so that our souls may dine leisurely at the feast of blessings found in God's presence. Jesus made clear that the discipline of Sabbath keeping as a law was meant for our well-being: "The sabbath was made for humankind, and not humankind for the sabbath" (Mark 2:27); and the greatest blessing provided for our well-being through the Sabbath is an increasingly deep enjoyment of the matchless presence of God.

The discipline of a day set aside for leisure in God has the additional benefit of gracing the following days of the week with the aroma of heaven. Sabbath keeping as a discipline strengthens our moment-by-moment sense of God, and as this grows it begins to permeate our workweek. We move from our Sunday day of rest in God into the spaces of Monday through Saturday, carrying God's presence with us into everyday life, and discovering that our commonplace routines are radically reinterpreted by having drunk deeply at the fountain of life. Instead of leaving

God's presence to return to "the real world," we discover that the Real World comes with us to help make sense of a world that has cut itself off from God.

While the discipline of Sabbath keeping certainly involves the discipline of worship, the latter is obviously not limited to one particular day a week. Indeed, we were created with worship of God as the central mandate of our lives. Hence time spent in the honor of God should undergird the remainder of our lives. As a spiritual discipline, worship can be exercised at any time, and has both corporate and individual aspects. Regular time alone before the divine throne reminds us that we belong utterly to God, who deserves our full attention and allegiance. Regular time together with God's people in worship reminds us that God's purposes are much larger than our individual lives, that he is God over all existence and our small part in the great drama of creation must fit within the grand design of our heavenly Father. Further, the discipline of corporate worship enables us to see the glory of God more fully than our private times allow. As we have already seen, the gifts of the Spirit are disseminated among all the people of God in the context of worship. No one individual exercises all the gifts, but in the event of corporate worship where the gifts are fully displayed, the character and activities of God are richly enjoyed through the Spirit-inspired ministries of fellow brothers and sisters. Worship deepens our humility by teaching us dependence on God and on one another in his name.

Prayer is the lifeblood of the interior Christian life, for it comprises our conscious, relational connection to God. Through prayer we nurture our walk with God, and are drawn more deeply into his mind and heart. Simply put, prayer is our primary form of communication with God, both in talking and listening. As every good relationship depends on free-flowing communication for growth and development, our life with God is no exception. The discipline of prayer, then, exposes us more fully to the God who loves to listen to us, but perhaps even more important, who loves to speak to us as well. After all, the incarnation trumpets this clearly; in the words of John, "The Word became flesh and dwelt among us" (John 1:14). As we grow in this spiritual discipline, we learn better how to listen to the often "still, small voice" of the Spirit, how to sense his will in the unfolding of events around us, how to gather up the yearnings of our hearts in petition, how to uncork the praise bottled up within our souls, how to wrestle with God over unresolved complaints, how to talk with him as a constant companion, in the cool of the garden, in the heat of the battles of life. While the disciplines of solitude and silence prepare us for prayer by stilling the cacaphony that often fills our mind, prayer's intent is to tune our ear to hear God's voice more clearly, and to respond appropriately to his summons.

Such discipline is necessary, for communication must be worked at in every relationship we wish to see grow. Many of us are all too familiar with "arrow prayers"—short communiques shot from our hearts or mouths heavenward in times of crisis or exultation: "Help, God!"; "Save us, Lord!"; "Whew! Thanks, God!" These kinds of prayer are wonderful in their place, but they are not enough to build a relationship upon. When we treat prayer as a daily discipline, we show our seriousness about wanting to nurture our life with God. Many Christians talk about wanting to have God more involved in their lives, but only those who work at developing the good habit of prayer demonstrate a desire that is more than lip service.

The discipline of study engages the mind in deeper love for God and others. As we dwell in a culture whose understanding of and approach to life is increasingly superficial, this discipline becomes all the more vital for Christians. We are called to have something substantive to say to the world, but if we ourselves are not steeped in the truth of God and its implications for life in the twenty-first century, our words will not be worth heeding. Study should first and foremost focus our attention on the Bible, which we confess to be the written Word of God. The quickest way to know the mind of God is to study his thoughts as revealed over three thousand years of history. The use of aids such as commentaries, atlases, Bible encyclopedias and dictionaries, lexicons and grammars will strengthen our grasp of the biblical text. Both reading slowly and intently for detail, as well as more quickly and broadly for the big picture, are invaluable parts of scriptural study. The discipline of study will also expose us to the writings of great Christian thinkers both contemporary and past. Works by authors such as Athanasius, Chrysostom, Augustine, Aquinas, Calvin, Luther, Wesley and Edwards expose us to theological perspectives from previous centuries and help inoculate us against the disease of chronological snobbery (as C. S. Lewis called it), the assumption that the issues we consider most important today and the explanations of life most in vogue at the moment are the only real ways to look at life. Contemporary Christian thinkers help us to probe more deeply the concerns of the present, but from angles that mainstream American thought often ignores.

Though study can be a solitary discipline, its benefits are magnified when pursued by a like-minded community, where the intellectual and practical insights of others deepen and enrich our own efforts. Surrounded by a culture interested in dumbing down the truth and beauty (see, for example, Allan Bloom's *The Closing of the American Mind*), and facing a church subculture that seems equally intent on avoiding the serious work of integrating a Christian worldview with the discoveries of secular disciplines (see Mark Noll's *The Scandal of the Evangelical Mind*), we are desperately in need of thinking Christians able to interpret the Reformed faith winsomely and thoughtfully to the larger world. To do this effectively will demand the discipline of study.

Linked closely with study is the discipline of meditation. Thinking well requires thinking deeply, and in Christian practice this is facilitated by the laserlike focus of mental energies upon a limited area of study, such as a verse of Scripture or a particular characteristic of God's nature or applications of a particular command of God. Unlike Eastern forms of meditation, where the object is to empty the mind of all conscious thought so as to merge consciousness with the Absolute Mind or to discover the unity of all existence, the discipline of Christian meditation seeks to fill the mind with one particular truth so as to explore all the contours of that claim, its ramifications for life and its place in the larger continuum of God's revelation. From Old Testament times, this practice has formed part of the interior life of God's people, as the Psalms in particular clearly show ("I will meditate on all your work, and muse on your mighty deeds" [77:12; see also 63:6; 77:3, 6; 119:15, 23; Josh. 1:8]). Unfortunately, the word "meditation" has been largely removed from the vocabulary of Christians due to its association since the 1960s with Eastern mystical practices, and many followers of Christ are ignorant of the biblical teachings on this subject. We need to reclaim our deep and vibrant heritage of mind and heart so as to plow deep furrows as we anticipate the transforming work of the Spirit.

Confession of sin, for many of us, is hardly a discipline. Rather, we engage in it only as a last resort, compelled by the unbearable guilt of conscience or by the public disclosure of our evils. Unpopular and painful as it is, however, the confession of sin is one of the disciplines of the Spirit, for it keeps our hearts from becoming callous toward God and his kingdom. Those who regularly confront the darkness of their hearts belong to the poor in spirit whom Jesus blesses in the Sermon on the Mount. They cry with the psalmist, "Search me, O God, and know my heart! Try me and know my thoughts! And see if there be any wicked way in me, and lead me in the way everlasting!" (Ps. 139:23–24). They know the promise conveyed through Psalm 51:17—"The sacrifice acceptable to God is a broken spirit; a broken and contrite heart, O God, you will not despise."

Confession indeed involves agreeing with God that our attitudes, intentions and behaviors have been wrong. So we often pray to God in community worship, "We have sinned against you in thought, word and deed." But confession demands the assent of our whole soul, not just the assent of mind and mouth. That is, confession without the willingness to turn away from the offenses we have committed against heaven is incomplete. Indeed, the words for "repentance" both in the Hebrew Old Testament and Greek New Testament underscore the act of turning away or changing from previous behaviors. In confession of sin, therefore, we not only recognize our wrong, but seek the grace of God and the accountability of the community to keep us from falling again into the same traps. This is one strong reason why the church down through the ages has seen confession as a discipline of the community; why James 5:16 commands us, "Therefore confess your sins to one another, and pray for one another"; and why the Reformation understood as one of its central teachings the priesthood of all believers. We are called to act toward one another in Christ's stead, serving as confessors for one another, and in his name offering the forgiveness won for us at the cross. Somehow, when the acts of hearing our confession and declaring God's pardon are incarnated through a brother or sister, they often are received by us with much greater impact than when we "retire to our closet" and pray in secret, just God and us in private. Secrecy here often leads us to the faulty belief that no one really knows what we are doing, and so we can keep on cultivating our sins and coming to God in private when the burden of our conscience grows too great, only to feel free to fall back into our old patterns upon concluding our prayer time. But when we have shared the shame of our hidden sins with fellow Christians who see us every day and with our permission can hold us accountable to God, we strip away the secrecy behind which evil flourishes, and lay the groundwork for the moral transformation of the Spirit, who seeks to conform us to the image of Christ.

The vulnerability and humility engendered by regular doses of confession free us to receive the Spirit's renewing work. As the power of sinful behavior is mitigated through our sincere confession and repentance, we find new space in our souls for the growth of virtue, planted by God. Jonathan Edwards was reputed to have said, "Nothing sets a person so much out of the devil's reach as humility." Indeed, the old saw, "Confession is good for the soul," proves true in a profound sense. As it is true for the individual soul, so it is good for the gathered body of Christ as well. Congregations that have jettisoned the prayer of confession and assurance of God's pardon in an attempt to appeal to the unchurched or to streamline the service (i.e., shorten it) are doing God's people and visitors a grave disservice. Where, if not in worship of the thrice-holy God, are we likely to be reminded of our sinfulness and need for redemption? Where, if not in the presence of the God of all mercy and comfort, are we likely to find the courage and honesty to expose the darkness within us to the light of God's countenance? Where, except in the worshipful gathering of fellow sinners soaked in God's grace, are we likely to find true community, based not on facade or human desire but on the cleansing and renewing acts of God made possible by the passion of Jesus Christ? Sadly, in the interest of drawing people to God some of our churches are removing from our communal worship experience the very things that enable us to honestly approach and know the God of the Bible, who demands holiness and nevertheless offers forgiveness.

This leads us rather nicely to the discipline of fellowship. Also spoken of as "community" or *koinonia* (the Greek word used of it in the New Testament), this practice involves much more than chatting about football or catching up on the latest news over coffee and donuts after church. The meaning of the root verb behind the word *koinonia* is "to share things in common, to participate together."

J. R. R. Tolkein's fantasy trilogy, *The Lord of the Rings,* opens with an account of Frodo Baggins, who has been chosen by a distant Providence to save all of Middle Earth, or perish in the attempt. He must carry Isildur's Bane, the One Ring of destiny, to Mount Doom, where it can be destroyed in the volcano's magma fires. Though Frodo alone must bear the ring, the wisest of counselors around him argue that he must not go alone, but a company should be appointed to assist him in this most critical task. Because of the incomparable magnitude of their common goal, the company swears allegiance to one another, pledging their lives to Frodo and the quest. Appropriately enough, this opening volume is entitled *The Fellowship of the Ring.* True fellowship is as weighty as the cause that binds participants together.

For Christians, *koinonia* entails the fellowship we share by being engrafted into the eternal life of Jesus Christ. We are linked together not simply by similar interests, viewpoints or even quests, but by participation together in the life of the Spirit made accessible by the sacrifice of the Son of God (see Eph. 2:11–22). When we speak of sharing fellowship together, we should take seriously the words of Paul in Ephesians 4:4–6: "There is one body and one Spirit, just as you were called to the one hope of your calling, one Lord, one faith, one baptism, one God and Father of all, who is above all and through all and in all." Times of "fellowship" for

Christians should be times when we are deepened in the common life we share in Jesus Christ. Coffee and donuts are great, but the cultivation of love that serves and edifies others, the shared compassion for a world lost in suffering and sin, the goal of glorifying Christ in all we say and do, the mutual quest of growth in the Spirit through practicing the disciplines of life together, these are what truly bind us together as brother and sister in the Lord. It is the Holy Spirit himself who fuses our lives together at the deepest level, that is, who makes us one by causing us to share the same essence of his life. Because of this unifying work of being, we can be unified in our doing as well.

Such fellowship is a precious gift to the people of God, and like all other divine gifts ought to be cultivated. This can happen to some degree as congregational members meet together on Sunday mornings, but typically there is neither time nor opportunity enough to share one another's lives deeply. Thus many Christians practice the discipline of fellowship by committing themselves to a small group of brothers and sisters who likewise yearn to learn more fully how to give their lives to one another and the world as a company of Jesus' disciples. There is not one set way of "doing small groups," but they will likely involve many of the communal disciplines outlined above—study of the Bible and Christian classics, prayer and worship together, perhaps confession and silence, experiments in fasting and evangelism. The purpose of such small groups, however, is not simply growing proficiency in certain spiritual disciplines, but growing together in our experience of God's love, which binds us as family to one another. Jesus' mission to our world entailed far more than the rescue of individuals. The kingdom of God that he revealed is characterized by family terms: brothers and sisters, Father and children. The full and perfect expression of these relationships (toward which the Spirit is training us) reflects the fulfillment of God's intentions toward the human race, as expressed in the law of Moses and summed up by Jesus: "You shall love the Lord with all your heart, mind and soul, and your neighbor as yourself." Community, in the Christian sense, is indispensable to the church. No Christian is meant to be an island in the world of God's kingdom. Hence the discipline of fellowship proves a vital means to our experience of life with Jesus Christ.

Lastly, we take up the discipline of service. Jesus calls his followers to a lifestyle of service, yet the world around us values being served more highly than serving.

> A dispute also arose among them as to which one of them was to be regarded as the greatest. But he said to them, "The kings of the Gentiles lord it over them; and those in authority over them are called benefactors. But not so with you; rather the greatest among you must become like the youngest, and the leader like one who serves. For who is greater, the one who is at the table or the one who serves? Is it not the one at the table? But I am among you as one who serves." (Luke 22:24–27)

How do we resist the constant lure of the world around us and our hearts within us to be lords over others? How do we ignore the categories of wealth, position, intellect, fame and power in the ways we evaluate people? How can we utilize our gifts and resources in the service of others, especially when our culture ignores or laughs or frowns upon our efforts to minister to those deemed "below us" in life? Jesus told what has become one of his most famous parables regarding whom we are to serve. Known as the parable of the Good Samaritan, it is our Lord's response to the evasive question, "Who is my neighbor?"[22] Jesus chooses as the hero of his illustration a Samaritan, one from a racial and religious class despised by Israelites. This good Samaritan fulfills the command of loving one's neighbor by caring for an assault victim he happens upon during his journey. The victim had already been noticed and avoided by two of Israel's religious elites—a priest and a Levite. The conclusion of the parable is that the neighbor we are called to serve in love is the person in need within our reach. But further, Jesus declares through this parable that it is the despised Samaritan who fulfills God's law, while the religious Jews of the story disobey this fundamental command of servant-hearted love. One of the dangers from which no person is immune, even (perhaps especially) religious persons, is the secret pride that weighs the worth of others on the basis of whether they are valuable enough to me to deserve my efforts. Jesus simply forbids this approach for his disciples.

The discipline of service trains us to see ourselves as those placed in this world by God to serve others. By taking steps to look for opportunities to help others in small and unobtrusive ways, we reorient our minds and wills from a focus on what we can get from others to one naturally poised to aid others however we can, as they are willing to receive our help in Christ's name.

The intent to serve others reflects the heart of the Son of God, who declared that he came "not to be served but to serve, and to give his life a ransom for many" (Mark 10:45). Since the ultimate goal of the Spirit's presence in our lives is to remake our fallen natures into the perfect human nature of the Son of God, our practice of this discipline of service will invariably fit the Spirit's intentions for our growth, and thus become a creative avenue for our sanctification in Christ.

Indeed, all of the above disciplines as well as many not mentioned here, when practiced out of faith in Christ and dependence on the grace of God, become creative channels of the life of the Spirit. Jesus promised all who believe in him that from within them springs of living water would flow (John 7:38, paraphrased). The full impact of this gift is experienced when we, like the Arabs of Hofuf, dig furrows to fully irrigate the surrounding countryside—in this case, the countryside of our heart. The green shoots portending a rich harvest of spiritual fruit cannot then be far behind.

It is such transformation that will characterize us as people of the Spirit, and testify to the reality of the Father's greatest gift to the human race through the redemptive work of his Son, the life of God himself residing in the Christian community and in the believer's heart. Not only does this endless supply of living water bring joy to our deepest lives, but he gives hope to a dry and thirsty world looking heavenward for some sign of relief. The church, the bride of Christ blessed with the gift of the Spirit, is called by God to display this new life and hope in its daily living, to point people to the Savior who dispenses living water to all who cry out for mercy. Jesus makes this free offer in Revelation 21:6: "It is done!

I am the Alpha and the Omega, the beginning and the end. To the thirsty I will give water as a gift from the spring of the water of life." And the Spirit himself through the witness of the church calls all with ears to hear, all who feel the thirst, to come and drink deeply:

> The Spirit and the bride say, "Come."
> And let everyone who hears say, "Come."
> And let everyone who is thirsty come.
> Let anyone who wishes take the water of life as a gift.
> (Rev. 22:17)

May the people of Christ live up to their calling, for the sake of the world, to the glory of the triune God!

Notes

1. The one exception to this is found in Jesus' cry upon the cross, when he quotes from Psalm 22, "My God, my God, why have you forsaken me?"
2. Mark makes especially clear in his Gospel that in the age of the Incarnation Jesus alone is the bearer of the Holy Spirit. Not even the disciples have direct access to the Spirit of God until after Jesus' atoning work is completed at the cross. Mark 13:11 promises a future empowerment for the disciples. After Jesus' resurrection, they will become inspired witnesses. But during his earthly life, the Spirit's work is focused entirely in and upon Jesus, so that there can be no mistaking the fact that in and through him alone is the Spirit of God found.
3. That each of Jesus' responses to the temptations comes from Deut. 6:13–8:3, a section of material dealing with Israel's own wilderness experience, points to the likely conclusion that Jesus had pondered deeply this portion of Scripture as he contemplated at the outset of his ministry the shape that his Father's call upon his life would take.
4. The Gospel accounts were not written in final form for many years after the church's formative experience of Pentecost, recounted in Acts 2. Though the inbreaking and continued indwelling of the Spirit proved to be an immensely powerful reality for Jesus' followers, it is a credit to the Gospel writers' historical faithfulness that they did not read back this reality into their accounts of the lives of Jesus' followers prior to Pentecost. Their clarity on the matter underscores even more the truth that the gift of the Spirit to the world is possible only upon the successful completion of Jesus' mission.
5. Jesus makes clear in John 14:17 that the disciples should recognize the Spirit, for in Jesus the Spirit dwells with them. But Jesus goes on to say that after he leaves them (by death), the Spirit will no longer simply be with them, but will now indwell them ("You know him, because he abides with you, and he will be in you").
6. It took the originally all-Jewish congregation of Jesus' followers a while for the impact of God's generosity toward "all" to sink in. Not until the Spirit was poured out on Gentile believers the same way it

had been poured out on Jewish believers (see Acts 10) did the apostles begin to see that God meant for the blessings of his redemption to be offered freely to all, regardless of race (Jew or Greek), sex (male or female) or social status (free or slave).

7. Known more technically as the "Diaspora," from a Greek verb meaning "to scatter," this group of Jews originated primarily as a result of Israel's captivity under the Assyrians and Babylonians. When the previously deported Jews were allowed by Persian king Cyrus to return from Babylon to their homeland, groups decided to stay where they had developed new roots, or to settle in communities along the route back to Judah. Later, under Greek rule numerous Jews were attracted to the intellectual and social trends of Hellenistic life, and naturally migrated toward the centers of such power. By the time of Rome's ascendance, there were gatherings (synagogues) of Jews in many of the major cities of the Greco-Roman world. Many of these communities had been in existence for centuries, comprised now of Jews who were fully acclimated to their adopted homeland, no longer speaking Hebrew or Aramaic as their mother tongue, and not as tied to Jewish cultural distinctives as their Palestinian ("native") counterparts.

8. The last part of Jesus' famous declaration concerning the church in Matthew 16:18 ("and the gates of hell [hades] will not prevail against it") has often been misconstrued. Readers often assume that Jesus meant the church will be assaulted by the forces of hell yet remain intact. However, Jesus speaks not of forces but of gates, the sites upon which invading armies would focus their attacks as the weakest point of a city's defensive wall. According to his imagery, the church is called to take the offensive, battering the gates of death and evil, which ultimately must fall to the Author of life and his army.

9. This is the central idea in Acts and the epistles behind the term "saint," which is the Greek noun related to the adjective "holy." To be a saint is not to have achieved some rarified level of spirituality, but rather simply to belong to Christ, to be set apart as his possession and yielded to his service.

10. A good friend of mine who worships from time to time in a particular Pentecostal church noted that though the structure of the worship was often free-flowing, the service nevertheless typically ended punctually at 12:15 p.m. "The Holy Spirit," he remarked with a grin, "must be pretty fastidious about time."

11. Such gifts were spoken of as "signs" initially with reference to the preaching of the gospel. Their supernatural power authenticated the message by demonstrating that God was with them in ways beyond natural human ability. Many today view sign gifts differently, not so much as a sign to the world of the truth of the gospel, but as a sign to believers of the reality of the presence of the Holy Spirit in their lives.

12. Charles Wesley, "And Can It Be."

13. *Aurora Leigh* (Oxford University Press: Oxford, 1993), book vii.

94 Notes

14. *Teaching a Stone to Talk* (San Francisco: Harper & Row, 1982), pp. 40–41.
15. C. S. Lewis, *The Lion, the Witch, and the Wardrobe* (Collier: New York, n.d.), chap. 8.
16. This is a literal translation of the Greek word *theopneustos*, typically translated "inspired by God," as in 2 Tim. 3:16, "All scripture is inspired by God. . . ."
17. This is an agricultural term in regular use in the ancient Mediterranean world, and found frequently in the Old Testament. It refers to the first production of vineyard, field or orchard, which served as harbinger of the greater yield to come. Metaphorically, it speaks of a small but significant start that promises a bountiful finale.
18. Such a perspective inevitably leads to a division of the body of Christ into first- and second-class believers, those who have the fullness of the Spirit and those who are still lacking that empowerment. Since few sincere Christians are willing to settle for being a "second-class" believer, the sign of speaking in tongues becomes a highly sought after experience, so much so that many seekers succumb to pressure (whether internal or external) and consciously or unconsciously manufacture the experience in order to be fully accepted by the congregation.
19. How interesting that Paul writes this verb "glorified" in the aorist tense in the original Greek. The tense typically indicates completed action in the past. Yet the glorification of Christians now living is definitely a future event. However, this divine accomplishment forms the final act of a series of events that have already occurred according to the undeniable force of God's will. Hence for Paul the final glorification of those in Christ is as certain as our call and justification, because God has willed it to take place. To emphasize this truth, he speaks of it as though already completed.

   That Paul means this is supported by his encouraging words to the Philippian believers: "I am sure that he who began a good work in you will bring it to completion at the day of Jesus Christ" (Phil. 1:6).
20. Though there were certainly many facets to Paul's apostolic ministry, Col. 1:29 makes clear that shaping the growing spiritual life of Christian communities was high on Paul's agenda. In Col. 1:29 he writes passionately, "For this [everyone's maturity in Christ] I toil and struggle with all the energy that he powerfully inspires within me."
21. The use of terms such as "exercise" and "training" is deliberate. Paul in particular is fond of using athletic and military metaphors to drive home the truth that the process of sanctification is akin to enrolling in the "gymnasium of the Spirit" or enlisting in "spiritual boot camp."
22. Asked by an expert in the law, this question sought to limit the scope of the command, "Love your neighbor as yourself," so that the lawyer in question, and the dodger of responsibility in all of us, could legitimize our unwillingness to care for those outside our narrow circles of relation. See Luke 10:25–37 for the full account.